The Journey of Healing

"When I was a teenager I used to stand in front of Monet's enormous painting of water lilies at the Modern Museum of Art in New York City and let my soul rest in the presence of all that beauty. After years of dreaming, I visited and photographed Monet's still-thriving garden in Giverny, France, where I took the cover photo of his water lilies."

—SABRINA FRANCESCA MANGANELLA

The Journey of Healing

WISDOM FROM SURVIVORS OF SEXUAL ABUSE

~A Literary Anthology~

Edited by Marjorie Ryerson
Photographs by Sabrina Francesca Manganella

The SaferSociety PRESS

Brandon, Vermont

Copyright © 2010 by The Safer Society Press, Brandon, Vermont
First Edition

"Awakening" by Susan Russell is reprinted with permission. Copyright © 2002 Civic Research Institute, Inc. This article was originally published in *Crime Victims Report,* Vol. 5, No. 6 (January/February 2002), pp. 87-88, and is reproduced here with permission.

"Healing Walks," "Risk the Dark," "Sometimes Angels," and "Wisdom's Past" are printed with permission. Copyright © 2010 M. E. Hart.

"Twelve" by Peter Wien is printed with permission. First appearance was in the videotaped session "How Men Can Act Against Violence Toward Women," by Dr. Raphael during the March 10, 2009 NGO Committee on the Status of Women conference in New York City.

"Freedom," by Forest Emily Franken, was previously published in a non-copyrighted chapbook titled *Shedding the Skin of Shame: Bearing Our Bodies' Truths.* The chapbook was put out by San Francisco Women Against Rape (SFWAR), 10/18/08, for an Artists Against Rape event.

Front cover photograph and interior photographs © Sabrina Manganella Simmons
Book design and composition by Cynthia Ryan
Printed in the United States of America
10 9 8 7 6 5 4 3 2 1

Library of Congress Cataloging-in-Publication Data

The journey of healing : wisdom from survivors of sexual abuse : a literary anthology / edited by Marjorie Ryerson ; photographs by Sabrina Francesca Manganella. -- 1st ed.
    p. cm.
ISBN 978-1-884444-86-9
1. Sexual abuse victims--Case studies. I. Ryerson, Marjorie.
RC560.S44J68 2010
362.883--dc22

2010011552

P.O. Box 340
Brandon, Vermont 05733
www.safersociety.org

The Journey of Healing: Wisdom from Survivors of Sexual Abuse
$15.00 plus shipping and handling
Order #WP142

Contents

ix   Preface

3   "We Are Everywhere," by Deb Sherrer

7   "Peas," by Larry Conrad

9   "What We Know," by Andrea Harris

15   "My Holocaust," by Yonina

19   "Healing Walks," by M. E. Hart

21   "I Stand," by Elizabeth McCurry

23   "My Street," by Dale Coleman

25   "Shattered," by Jennifer Majesky

27   "Eleven Years," by Kitty Garn

29   "Four O'Clock," by Richard G.

35   "Boundaries," by Jolie McKenna

37   "The Trial," by Julia Vileisis

41   "Twelve," by Peter Wien

47   "The Night to Remember," by Ahn Pearl

49   "Awakening," by Susan S. Russell, M.A.

55   "The Reporter: The Whole Story"

59   "My Wounded Warrior," by Dale Coleman

63   "The Rape," by Kitty Garn

67   "Carved in Stone," by Jon

69   "The Road Back," by Marcia

73   "The Abyss," by Linda Schritt

75   "Risk the Dark," by M. E. Hart

79   "Susan," by Rebecca

85   "diligent suns," by S. Kelley Harrell

87   "Moving Day," by Catherine and her 12-year-old daughter

89   "Our Stories," by Mitzi Soto Albertson

91   "Vulture," by Dale Coleman

93   "How I Learned to Swim," by Desmonette Hazly, Ph.D.

99   "Beauty that is," by Beth Smith

101   "Anger," by Sabrina Francesca Manganella

107   "fighting cholitas," by Liz Cascone

113   "Bitter for the Sweet Child Within," by Nazneen Tonse

115   "Up from the Ashes," by Kathy

119   "Returning Home," by Jackie

123   "Sometimes Angels," by M. E. Hart

125   "The Forest of Life," by Sara

129   "Knees," by Paula Hodgkins

131   "Shrapnel," by Deb Sherrer

133   "Grooming," by Mary Zelinka

141   "I'm Telling," by Donna

149   "Day in Court," by Nick

153   "Thank You, George," by Larry Conrad

159 "Sunshine and Rainbows," by Lorraine

161 "Nature's Healers," by Pamela Brendel

163 "There Is Hope in Healing," by R.

169 "I Promised the Children," by Earthlake

173 "The Unrelenting Optimist," by Carlene

177 "In My Own Skin," by Melanie Cleary

179 "Curling Clouds," by Vikram

183 "standing naked," by Hadiyah Carlyle

187 "The Best Boy," by Dale Coleman

189 "Freedom," by Forest Emily Franken

191 "Rebirth," by Bryanna Houston

195 "I Am From," by Cynthia

197 "Wisdom's Past," by M. E. Hart

201 About Our Contributors

209 Resources

Preface

The 56 stories and poems in this anthology were written by a geographically and culturally diverse group of exceptionally talented and caring individuals. On the following pages, these writers have generously, artfully, and intimately shared their personal experiences of and recovery from sexual violence. Their writings represent a small portion of hundreds of other equally moving pieces submitted for possible inclusion in this book, writings we were unable to include here principally due to space limitations, but also occasionally due to underlying legal restrictions. Regardless, all of these voices—those in this book and those yet to be published— are voices that must be heard.

Each time such violence happens to one single person, we all need to be asking why such a crime has been committed. We also need to ask why sexual violence happens to so many people, and what we can do to stop it from happening. Information specialists who gather statistics about this topic tell us that approximately a third of all females and a sixth of all males experience personal sexual violence during their lifetimes. Those numbers, when looked at globally, add up to nearly two billion citizens of both genders, citizens representing all races, nationalities, ages, cultures, and political and personal philosophies. Adding even greater weight to the magnitude of this tragedy is that these high numbers are actually misleading because many people affected by sexual violence—perhaps even a majority—respond by choosing a lifetime of silence. Such numbers indicate that we are bearing witness to an individual and a human tragedy of incomprehensible global proportions.

In April 2009, when I first put out a call for literary writings for this anthology, I had no idea contributions would pour in not only from all over the United States, but also from many regions of the world. By the submission deadline, in mid-August, I had received hundreds of poems, plays, fiction stories, songs, and essays from five continents and from nearly every state in the United States. I had clearly underestimated the power of the Internet, the effectiveness of the one listserver to which I belonged, and the reach of ten or twelve professional colleagues to whom I had spoken about the book, including the staff at The Vermont Approach at the University of Vermont. The credit for the success of this book's creation, however, must, *most of all,* be directly extended to the willingness of all those contributors who heard about the book and who chose to send their writings in to our press.

Some of the writers appearing in these pages asked to have their pieces published under just their first names, to allow for privacy. Others felt it was important to speak their whole truth aloud, fully identified, while also specifically naming their abusers. As legal issues were identified, the nuances of these issues were discussed with each author, and we collectively worked out the best solutions we could find to allow the writers' stories to be honest and complete while also avoiding possible libel charges. Some of the authors whose works appear only under their first names, including Donna and Carlene, would have liked to have shared their full identity in the book but were unable to because of legal constraints.

My work in assembling this book was closely and invaluably supported through-out the year-long process by freelance editor Collette Leonard, who ably helped with all stages of preparation and production. Collette's meticulous and sensitive talents have been invaluable as have been the creative and supportive skills of book designer Cynthia Ryan. Thanks are also extended to the staff and board members of Safer Society for their ongoing assistance with and belief in this project. Most of all, I wish to extend thanks and gratitude to the international collection of writers, and the art photographer, whose work is included here, and to all others who sent in stories, songs, and poems for consideration. These voices are the true inspiration behind the creation of this book.

It is my fervent hope that *The Journey of Healing* reaches out into the world to embrace those affected by abuse, those wishing to further educate themselves and others about the topic, and those hoping to decrease the incidence of such violence. None of us—regardless of our own life experiences—are immune from this topic. Our responsibility is to listen respectfully and well to these voices and to do every-thing we can to end this human tragedy.

—Marjorie Ryerson

The Journey of Healing

We Are Everywhere

by Deb Sherrer

caring for small children
leading business meetings
volunteering at schools, hospitals, the local rape crisis center
writing best selling novels

our stories vary in detail
one was raped by a stranger in a dark parking lot
the stereotypical image of sexual violence
while another was molested by her father or neighbor or family friend
the language changes, but the facts are essentially the same
someone used force or coercion to overpower, abuse, shame
and the healing takes years

but we go on
skillfully, courageously
often silently
we are your colleagues, neighbors, friends
and you might never know
because such stories rarely have a place
in daily conversation

and we go on
sighing at every new magazine article
that offers women
yet more advice
on how to lose weight, dye our hair, diminish signs of aging

dress more confidently/sexily/fashionably
be somehow other than what we are
who we've become
like somehow we never get it right
which is ultimately what rape taught us
especially when the voices start rattling in our heads

if only
we had fought back
never gone on the date
told our mother, guidance counselor, minister
not worn *that* particular outfit
chosen another way home, a different man to partner with
not taken the candy, the balloon, the offers of kindness

but no

if only
we, as a society, could STOP
gorging ourselves
on a daily diet of violence against women
the endless stream of print ads
selling stuff-sex-women-stuff-sex-women
the nightly TV dramas
movies and magazines
fantasy or supposed parody
portraying what is only
too real

if you know one woman who has been raped or battered
and trust me, you probably do
don't buy a movie ticket to see

a woman beheaded in front of her daughter
shut off your TV in protest
of violent content as entertainment
tell Nike to shove their ads
and their products
when they dare to depict a woman
in running sneakers
fleeing from a man with a chain saw

the one that got away

because many more of us didn't
and we are your colleagues, neighbors, friends

we are everywhere

Peas

by Larry Conrad

"Larry, could you pass the peas, please?"
My mother's words startle me at first and
I realize where I am – and it's suppertime.
How did I get home? How did it end today?
I'm so afraid and I'm hurt bad – again.

I'm staring out from deep inside my eyes.
It's like watching a movie, only up close,
Examining them as they enjoy their dinner,
Talking about how their day has been in
The steady tones that mean they are safe.

Colors and smells, sounds, this chair hurts.
My mouth is making words that aren't mine.
My fork feels heavy and I stare into my plate
From my dark and chaotic world, where my
Cries plead for help but never make a sound.

Would they love me if they knew the truth?
Could they bear to look at his "lovely boy"?
I know that even now he could still slip in
And drag me away screaming in the night
And no one would see, no one would hear.

An eternity seems to pass as the storm crashes
And wells from deep within – I can't stay here.

I so want it all to stop, and in a moment I feel
Myself drifting away, free for a time, leaving
The boy, as he passes the peas to his mother.

What We Know

by Andrea Harris

My father is a professional hospital visitor. The clergy badge clipped on the mirror in his pickup truck grants him access to even those rooms where death holds the machine wires in its bony fingers. For over 40 years he has been comforting the sick, the dying, the lonely, and the left-behind. It's his job to minister. I am constantly amazed by his ability to say just the right words—the words that make people feel like everything will be okay. But that morning he had no words. He sat in the hall outside the examination room while strangers took samples from my body, and he silently put his gray head in his hands. The one room his clergy badge could not get him into was the room in which a rape kit was being done on his daughter. That morning he had no words.

Accustomed to late-night calls for help, he had answered the phone without panic.

"Andrew Brewster."

"Dad, I was raped. I'm driving to the police station," I heard my voice say. When the words were done, I hung up. It was all I was capable of saying. I had pressed the numbers on my cell phone purely by instinct. The childish need to tell Daddy someone had hurt me was stronger even than the fear that the man who raped me was still watching me.

The rape had stripped me of all adult pretensions. My belief in autonomy and control had come off with my purple sweater and black pants. Hours later, when he was done, he watched me dress and asked why I put my pants on inside out. I told him it didn't matter because I was just going home. I thought putting them on inside out would be good evidence when I went to the police. He did not ask why I left my autonomy and control on the floor in his bedroom. Maybe he liked the thought that they would stay there with him, guaranteeing my return to his bedroom over and over again.

I entered the police station and collapsed. Someone came out and talked to me as I huddled on the floor underneath the counter. I remember he had kind eyes and didn't touch me until I said it was okay. When my father got there, I was sitting in a chair in the back. People were talking all around me. No one could get me to respond. The words "traumatized," "shock," "hospital," and "raped" zoomed in and out of my consciousness like tiny, persistent sweat bees; I resisted the urge to swat them. As the medics loaded me into the back of the ambulance, I heard my father ask if he should ride with me.

I had always wondered what it would be like to ride in an ambulance, to go screaming down the street through red lights and intersections. I still wonder. The next thing I remember after being loaded into the ambulance is lying on an examining table. A male doctor was telling me what he would be taking from my body. I could see my father in the hallway whenever someone opened the door to enter or leave.

The nurse was excited when a single tear rolled down my cheeks. "She's coming out of it!" she told my father.

But I wasn't, not really. I was crying because my father looked so small and helpless sitting out there in the hall. He looked so sad, and they would not let me climb off the table to go to him.

A few years after the rape, I walked into my father's den when he was watching *Law and Order: Special Victims' Unit.* The detectives were trying to get a young woman to talk about being raped. I stopped on my way to the kitchen and stared at the young girl on the screen. My father changed the channel. The rape remains largely unspoken between us. I do not want my father to know I was given a choice between sucking a man's penis and having his penis shoved in my anus. I do not want him to know which I chose. I do not want him to know the choice was a deception, that a hand was forced through my anus anyway. Most of all, though, I do not want him to know that the man who did these things told me he would send the pictures he was taking of me to my father's church if I told anyone. I still worry about those pictures, even though the police assured me the camera was only a toy. I do not want my father to see the pictures. Yet, I know, when my father switches the channel from *Special Victims' Unit* to football, he does so in part because he already sees those pictures and just doesn't want me to know.

My son William is a kind and thoughtful boy, wise for his age. We are very close, my Spud and I. When I was lying on that bed, the man on top of me promised that if I stopped struggling he would take the pillow off and let me breathe. I refused to stop struggling. I decided to let him kill me. If he still wanted my body when all the breath was gone from it, he could have it. I left my body and sat in a corner of the room, watching the struggle. Then I saw my son, tottering with still unsteady steps toward me, arms upheld, wanting me to pick him up. And I remembered. Remembered William would wake up in the morning and want me to hold him. I got up from the corner and walked to my son. As my arms went around his chubby little body, I was back on the bed. I stopped struggling, stopped screaming. And the pillow was taken off.

When William was 10 years old, a famous man was accused of rape. William noticed my reaction to the news coverage but did not question me about it. We had already talked about sex several times, but I wasn't sure if he knew what rape was.

As I tucked him into bed one night, he startled me by blurting out, "Rape is when a man hurts a woman, right? Like beats her up and stuff?"

"Yes and no. Rape is when a man forces a woman to have sex with him." I responded to what he already knew, consciously choosing to leave out how men rape other men, men and women rape children, children rape other children, and, in rare cases, women rape men.

"So he beats up the woman just to have sex with her?"

"Sometimes, William. Sometimes he threatens her, and the woman has sex with him because she is scared and wants to save her life or avoid being beaten up. Sometimes the woman is just so shocked by what is happening that her body and mind shut down."

He nodded slowly, and then asked, "When a woman is telling the truth about being raped, she always goes to court, right?"

"Not always. Going through a rape trial can be just as painful as being raped." I was careful here, feeling for the line into dangerous territory. "When people don't believe the woman has been raped, they try to make her look crazy or like she is a bad person."

"You mean like she deserved it?"

I nodded, surprised by how quickly he caught on.

Before I left his room, he asked me one last question: "Mom, do you believe that woman on the news who says she was raped?"

"What I know is that women who are raped need to be believed," I told my son. "I was raped when you were little, and no one wanted to believe me. So I know how bad it feels not to be believed."

I was at the door when I heard his voice. "I'm sorry, Mom."

Almost 10 years after William saved my life, his recreational basketball team included two girls. After the first practice, he told me, "Don't worry, Mom. I know from you how good girls can play, and I'll be just as tough with them as I am with the guys."

I have always tried to be strong in front of my son, to show him the strength of being a woman. He does not remember that Christmas so many years ago when Mom locked herself in her room. He doesn't know about the years when he was my only light and the rest of my life was in darkness, and I don't want him to know. I don't want him to know how little I respected myself. I don't want him to know what I did to avoid the risk of saying "No." Because he thought I was strong, I became strong again. Because he believed in me, I learned to believe in myself again. He has saved my life twice. He doesn't know that now, but one day I'll tell him.

The man who raped me is named James. I was not the first or the last woman he raped. He was very smart about the rape. He knew how to set it up so that witnesses could lend credibility to his story. He knew how to get me alone. He knew what to say to get me to comply. He even knew what to tell the cops when they arrested him. The only thing he didn't know was that I was lying when I promised I would not go to the police. He is in jail now, and I wonder how often he regrets the decision to let me leave that night. I wonder if he is planning to come fulfill his promise to kill me and my son when he gets out of jail. He is not in jail for my rape alone. Raping me after the work holiday party is just a tiny blip on his criminal record, a blip that wouldn't even be there if I hadn't given the prosecutors so much hell. I wonder if he knows about that, too.

I was lying there, but I wasn't there. I was somewhere else. I didn't feel his penis inside my vagina or my mouth until days later, when I would wake up screaming, thinking I was being raped again. I didn't even feel the ripping of my anus from his hand until the next day, when I tried to have a bowel movement and screamed. I had completely disconnected from my body.

So when he told me I was beautiful, the words just waited in my head for my return.

As I sucked on his limp penis and tried to make it hard so that he could rape me better, he moaned, "God, you are beautiful."

Why didn't I bite down? Because I knew it wouldn't kill him; it would just make him angry. And he had already proven he was faster and stronger than me. I knew I wouldn't make it out of the house and to my car in the driveway.

While he was thrusting himself inside me, he told me again, "You are beautiful." And after he ejaculated, he caressed my breasts and said, "I love you. And you love me. We're going to be together now. You're going to have my baby."

It has been over 10 years since the man who raped me told me he loved me. Those three words are the words I remember most often. Not the "You're not leaving until I fuck you." Not the "Dick or ass. Suck my dick, or you get it in the ass." Not the "If you don't try harder, I'm going to get on the phone and call all my buddies over." Not the "I'm going to send these pictures to your dad's church, his home, and that college you go to." Not even the "If you tell anyone, I will kill you and your son. I know where you live." No, the words that still haunt me after all these years are "I love you," "You're beautiful," and "We're going to be together now." But I don't want him to know that. I don't want him to know I still cringe whenever a man, even a man I love, tells me I'm beautiful or how much he loves me. I don't want the man who raped me to know these things, to know that he is still in me. But I am afraid that he already knows. I am afraid that's *why* he did it.

My Holocaust

by Yonina

I sit
curled up
on my dining room chair
my feet up on the seat
arms around my knees
chin resting on them

it's the 7th day of Passover
my family sits around the table
my grandfather has the floor
he sits directly across from me
telling stories...
of Pain
Suffering
atrocities beyond imagining

the Hunger that clawed deeper than talons
the Fear
deep Fear
of every second
being Pursued
Hunted
no rest...

and I sit there
drinking in all that pain

wondering how a person could live through all that
...and come out Sane
Alive
Functioning
Happy
Fulfilled...
I wonder how I can ever relate,
me, in my comfortable house,
with everything I ever need
no hunger
no Nazis
no fear

and then...
as I sit there...
indeed...the Fear...

the Feelings...come clawing in
the Fear
deep Fear
of every second
being pursued
Hunted
no rest...

it's not my grandfather's Holocaust
just...a personal holocaust
being hunted down by memories
haunted by phantom sensations
during the day
the night

in class
at weddings
family dinners
any time...any place
the constant anxiety...Fear

the holocaust that never goes away
that's not talked about
that's hidden from everyone
the secret that stays locked inside me
that my family doesn't even know about...
I can't talk about it like my grandfather does
he can share
he can talk
I cannot
it is my secret...
my personal Nazi...standing over me...

through my haze...
I'm brought back to the present
he's still talking
still telling his stories

he looks my way
reaches over and pats my arm in a loving way
says, "My sweet girl...you are so lucky...
you have not suffered such things..."

I have not.

but...have I not?

Hunger
...for the Truth...
to be saved...
...loved...
Fear...so deep
the claws...sharp talons
...of self-doubt and self-hatred and anger and frustration...

I *have* suffered.

and I still do.

yet...I think...of his stories
they went through all that hell
and they came out.

like my grandfather,
I will come through it
Sane
Alive
Functioning
Happy...

Fulfilled.

one day.
I will get there...

I believe it.

Healing Walks

by M. E. Hart

Healing walks
It does not run
It rises slowly with the morning sun
Floats lightly on the morning breeze
Whispers its mantra through the rustling trees

Healing walks with the shimmering brook
Flowing over mountains through winding crooks
Crooks and crannies
Twists and turns
Healing walks
It does not yearn

The trees and flowers drink it in
And then quietly breathe it out again
It floats on the breath that each plant makes
Riding the air that we will soon take

Healing walks through us
As we take it in
In some it will rest
In some it will end

And with a heat of blazing fire
Healing comforts and warms
Holding life gently in loving arms

Healing walks
It does not swoon
Even in the light of the blue full moon
It rides the waves of the blue moon beams
It travels freely where each beam gleams

Healing walks
It does not run
It travels the path with
Moon and Sun
   Wind and Fire
      Snow and Rain

Healing walks without shame
Unafraid in the face of love
Unafraid of a caring hug
Unafraid of pain and bliss
Healing walks, softly, like a gentle kiss

Walk with open mind and heart
You don't want to miss this!

I Stand

by Elizabeth McCurry

I feel the weight of the world bear down on my shoulders
as the complications of life sweep my feet from under me,
the impact so great and the hurt so bad that it's hard to stand back up,
but yet I stand.
They laugh and call me names ripping out my heart and tossing it to
    the side like garbage.
Taking every chance they get to tear me apart,
but yet I stand.
I fight the demons in my head trying to remain sane.
The fight takes all the strength I have,
but yet I stand.
The storm rages against me and my cheeks become wet.
The wind blows me back even though I try to move forward,
So, I stand.
The pain stabs me in the heart like a knife and my soul shatters into a
    million pieces.
Desperation takes me over,
but still I stand.
He took my innocence ripping it from me during the night.
My life changed forever,
But still I stand.

My Street

by Dale Coleman

When I was four
I lived
On a street named
FATE
Which my new neighbor
Soon would
Create

When I was five
I lived
On a street named
FEAR
There is no safe place
When the predator
Lives near

When I was six
I moved
To a street named
PAIN
Those feelings that lingered
Even now
Still remain

When I was seven
I moved
To a street named
SHAME
Such a young boy
Made to play
In his game

When I was eight
I moved
To a street named
GUILT
So much confusion
In all the ways
That I felt

When I was nine
I moved
To a street named
SAD
The way I still feel
Whenever the memories
Are had

Shattered

by Jennifer Majesky

I was made shattered.
A ruined soul now exists
where a whole person
once
was.

I break plates and glasses,
smashing them for release;
The fractured pieces litter the floor
and I can't help but relate
to each broken fragment.

I'm the broken vase that lies on the floor,
the spilled water decorating the tile
with the tattered roses
begging for
life.

The body is soft and supple,
able to absorb   blows.
Identities are fragile
and difficult to repair.
My self is destroyed.

I've put the pieces back together with glue—
that's progress—

but the glue is still curing and the pieces
don't fit together quite right.

I am not okay.

We work with
available light
to mend the fractured soul.
Like plates, I am the

product of human efforts.

You made me shatter.

Eleven Years

by Kitty Garn

The rape
Was the easy part.
What's so trying for me now
Are the days, the weeks, the years; undoing a mental picture of myself
That for all the outward loveliness is so inwardly ugly to me.
And the punishment, the purgatory of loving the haters;
My penance for an act I could not stop.

I was sleeping when it happened
From the poison I had poured down my throat
But the vomit on my shirt was not enough of a distraction
To stop them from taking me,
With every thrust and jab replacing me,
With this woman who cries for no reason,
Who fears for no reason,
Who trusts for no reason,
Who loves for no reason,
Who needs for no reason.
But to see the girl I was one more time.
To *feel* the girl I was before

The rape

Was the easy part.
What's so trying for me now
Is not liking the dark, not liking to sleep; drinking more than every man

In this room and still standing because I will forever be
The last to close my eyes only after I'm sure
Everyone else is sleeping.

If I could just see that girl one more time,
I would tell her that I love her.
I would say good-bye.

Four O'Clock

by Richard G.

For my Artist Way Group,
Desiree, Kevin, Lisa, Loretta, and Marcia,
whose support was so necessary
for me to write this story.

It is four o'clock in the morning and I am uncomfortably sitting in my bed. Wide awake again like every morning for the last five years, exactly at the same time, four o'clock, I woke up with the same panic in my chest, right in the heart of my heart. The fragile organ feels like it is being pulled apart in all directions.

In spite of the evident action taking place right in the middle of my chest, only tonight do I seem to have become able to identify the source of the discomfort and pinpoint the area of my body where a terrible and brutal combat, responsible for the abrupt interruption of my sleep for all those years, is happening.

I now resort to slowly brushing my right hand over my heart, drawing deliberate circles the size of a softball until I reach the number one hundred. Dr. Jing, an acupuncturist I was referred to by a good friend, convinced that I had too many things going on in the head, had suggested the nocturnal practice. As I reach one hundred, I reverse the movement and draw the same number of circles in the opposite direction. I have to say that after many nights obliging the good doctor, I am still not quite sure what the effect of the circles is supposed to be. What I know is that now I am totally exhausted on top of being wide awake. I am now completely extenuated. Oh so tired...

Tonight it is becoming pretty obvious that the place that is too full is my heart. There are too many things going on in my heart! That's what I could have told Dr. Jing. I have a lot of things present in there. What I could also have told the acupuncturist is that at around four o'clock every morning, all those things get activated;

my heart becomes this arena where some of those things want to hatch and leave, others bounce stubbornly against the walls and refuse to circulate, and others throw themselves blindfully against whatever they find just so they get some kind of attention. Others simply need to assert themselves and shout obscenities. The resulting chaos feels, for the poor sleeper that I am, like a wrestling match where none of the contestants, all very strong, very healthy, and well trained, will concede or go down for the count.

It is four twenty-six. I finally decide to identify the fighters present in my heart, so I can line them up and face them one by one in the ring. I am not sure if I really want a real fight or just a great opportunity to run away and leave them free rein. One thing is for sure: when daylight comes, I will need my heart. I want my heart to be free and available for all those upcoming moments today: I might need it to resist judging a friend who said something I found offensive, or later on, to smile at the man at Starbucks who's so adorably adding milk to his coffee and who could become my life partner; or this afternoon, when I send a resume to a future employer, I might need my heart to do that task with gentleness and compassion for myself. I want my heart free now. It is four thirty-two and it is not one minute too soon for me to get in there. I am ready for the brawl! Watch out.

OK! Who is there? I close my eyes (they are so red, it hurts!). I slowly bring my attention to the center of my chest. My heart feels so huge now it seems to occupy most of the cavity. There is screaming and kicking in there and yet I keep breathing, as slowly and fully as I can. Somehow I am convinced I can do that. With firm resolution, I take another breath. And another breath...inhale...exhale. Inhale...exhale. The mattress feels softer. And suddenly, I am not sure I want to go any further. I am afraid. All my muscles are tightening up.

Somehow I suspect I know exactly who I am going to find; it might be better for me to leave at this point. I am somehow familiar with those silhouettes. I want to stop breathing, I want to stop writing. Why do I want to do this? Why would I do this? It is just going to make them angrier.

Let's turn the TV on as usual and let's get a good dose of infomercials. Oh! That would feel so good: all my pans could be extra-clean, I would finally be able to flatten my belly, all in 15 minutes, and I would have the lightest vacuum cleaner of anybody in the street. I want a flat belly! The fighting becomes more intense. I can feel all the heavyweights throwing themselves into the ropes and bouncing off each other. A couple of guys are climbing the third rope and jumping off while landing on whomever is passing by. The pain is extreme, yet so subtle.

I take a deeper breath, my eyes still closed. As I watch the air going out, I notice I suddenly have the choice not to clench my jaw. That is good news for my bottom teeth, which are almost gone by now from the nocturnal grinding. Another slow breath. I feel my whole spine letting go of the pull I usually apply to it. I did that? Wow! Could I actually have the choice not to clench my jaw and leave my spine alone? What a pleasant sensation! More room for me to breathe. I breathe more deeply and take pleasure at repeating the process. It is four fifty-six and I feel surprisingly more alive. It sounds like a paradox at this point. I decide to keep going within. I use the newfound spine to guide me down toward the cavity. I jump from one vertebra to another, almost joyously.

I realize that I know who those fighters are, and I really don't want to talk to them, wrestle them, or even look at them. I know them from a long, long time ago. My heart is beating faster, very fast. Can a heart really explode? Here, this morning? Before I can feel sadness, I become unbelievably enraged. I am so angry! And then, I become angrier because I'm so angry. I am so angry. God, I am angry. All those years. I can't believe they did that to me. I can't believe he did that to me. I feel the anger, but I also feel the terror.

I think of my heart: pounced on, bruised, lacerated, and withered. I feel more sadness taking hold in my body. A faint smile appears in the back of my throat. Air is coming in again, through the nostrils usually obstructed by some deviation. I start breathing again. In...out...in...out. I sense I am finally arriving at the end of this long and difficult descent. I pause for a second and my undertaking, at this minute, feels more, from here, like a pilgrimage, a long overdue trip intended to accomplish some kind of ritual. A sense of deep satisfaction overtakes me as I start almost playfully exploring the new landscape. I feel like I have been preparing for this journey for all these years. I relax the space between my eyes. There I go, all the way to my heart.

I had expected the walls to be reddish and smooth. I am baffled to find a labyrinth of deep purple folds and double folds where the flesh turns on itself two or three times and forms dark caves or chambers, suitable to hold some kind of deposit. The general shape of my heart has nothing to do with the description found in anatomy books I had in college, nor with the image implied in some of the novels I have read. The lobes are facing the same direction and are separated by some kind of huge appendix, the whole thing forming a sort of crucible, fitted with a multitude of miniature chambers.

I can hear distorted sounds coming out of some of the folds. I get close to a disproportionately large one on my left. There are definite sounds coming out of this mound of flesh. Words are at first inaudible but as I focus on the source, I can hear a voice. It is the voice of my mother, muffled by the overgrown purplish flesh. "No matter what, he's your father," the voice says. I fall to the ground and find myself at the bottom of the cavity. Through an interstice, I recognize my mother. She is standing at the kitchen window, busy as usual watching and commenting on the comings and goings of cars in a parking garage across the backyard, as she tries to avoid looking at us sitting at the kitchen table. Her skin is green, her nose capped with a huge bump. I look at her with anger. She sees me: "I really don't know what happened to this one; he used to be so gentle."

From a fleshy bulge to the right, new images are surfacing. I see my sister scolding me for not doing enough to keep my father from drinking. I am 12; she is 14 in the image. She keeps insisting I go caddy for my father so he does not drink as much after his game of golf. I am terrified. I am terrified of him. Once the images are gone, I can hear her yell, "I hate you." As the voice fades, it leaves tiny water droplets behind each syllable. The next image to emerge is myself, shattered. My heart is shattered. I take a deep breath.

As I further explore the lineaments of my heart, I discover a large, very dark, tight nodule that seems to be connecting to some kind of artery: I instantaneously know I am facing what I came here for. Twelve years ago, after a strenuous but very powerful private yoga lesson, as I am lying on my back in the "corpse" pose, I am assailed by shocking images: I am witnessing the rape of a small boy by an older man. The infant is lying on his back on a table and the man is penetrating the small body with force and abandon. I don't understand. I see the man's eyes and he is looking at me, me on the studio floor, and me now. I see the little body and I am looking at myself. I feel my back, totally inert and frozen, and I feel his back totally inert and frozen, paralyzed. I am paralyzed. I don't understand. My teacher, whom I trust deeply, urges me not to judge anything but to observe. I am left flabbergasted.

Years later, as we are traveling in the winter, my father, my mother, and I, the storm is raging and I suggest to my father, who's driving, that we turn around and take the highway instead of the already very slippery small road. He immediately starts yelling at me. He's been driving for 50 years and I won't start telling him what to do and how to do things. I reply that if it is like this, I prefer not to go. I ask him to stop the car so I can get off and go back home. He refuses to stop the car and keeps going. I try to open the door but the door is locked. I ask him again to stop the car. He yells that he's going to show me who's in charge here. He yells at me as he keeps driving. That's the man! I recognize the violent manners, the way the space is occupied by the raging person around me, the odor, the crazy eyes! That's him! That's the man. My mother, in the backseat, keeps begging me to stay here and go "for her." She keeps repeating, "Richard, do it for me, do it for me." I want to vomit. I start kicking the door, the window, and the windshield with uncontrollable force. The man, my father, stops the car. By now, it feels like a déjà vu. I am reliving a nightmare all over again; the man, my father, is on top of me and won't let go, as my mother is making sure I'll go with it.

Inhale...exhale. Deep breath. I am indeed in front of what I came here for, facing it. Using my breath, I review all the images emanating from my heart. My breath is the least obstructed it has ever been. It feels light. Lightness. I stare at the nodule, as tears come from my eyes.

I notice a change in the dark bulge. It slowly starts to dissolve. The color of the flesh is changing and getting lighter. Who did that? What is happening? All the folds are also slowly unraveling themselves and revealing their insides and their secrets, reminding me of flowers, blossoming.

As I witness this amazing unwrapping, I suddenly become aware of who had fabricated these folds, a long time ago. The folds were made necessary in my body so

I would not have to hate those people. I did not want to hate, and I had fabricated the folds; my heart, as a crucible, had volunteered to host those events until I had the strength to come and attend to the fire that would produce the alchemy able to transform and nourish me. I did not want to hate, and the doughty and fearless organ knew exactly how to protect me.

Once this thought goes through my mind, I see each and every one of the folds open completely and let go of a beautiful gold butterfly. Soon my heart is filled with the golden fluttering of dozens of diaphanous wings. The walls slowly take a beautiful shade of deep red, mixed with blue, full of life and vibrancy. The fluttering transforms itself into a light and very rapid vibration. After hitting off the walls of the now glowing organ, the vibration becomes so strong that it crosses the pericardium and spreads quickly to the diaphragm and to my whole torso. There is some kind of joyous dance happening inside of me and I start smiling. My mid-back, inert and frozen for so many years, is now opening up to let air in between the shoulder blades. Pretty soon my whole body is engulfed in a radiant blaze as each cell of my body bathes in a golden light. It is five thirty. The exhaustion leaves, to be replaced by an extraordinary sensation of freshness. I am slowly falling asleep. The smooth walls of my heart are pulsing in a slow and regular beat, each cell of my body finally resting.

And my belly is flat.

Boundaries

by Jolie McKenna

I said no today
I'll say it again tomorrow
I am stronger now
You cannot tell me not to have salad
After I've eaten my meal
You cannot tell me how to cut my hair

Nations have borders
They get to decide who they let in
And who they keep out
People are like that too
I'm going to be a border guard
I'm going to be the customs official

And when you try to cross my line
With your radioactive toxin
And your drugs
I will have dogs that will tear you down
You will pee your pants
I will be doing my job

I'll go home at the end of a day
Have a drink with my friends
Laugh a little
Watch a movie
Go to bed
The next day I will still be the border guard

The Trial

by Julia Vileisis

He was engulfed by her beauty. Her light brown hair fell into wonderful, perfect pin-curls. Her face held just the right amount of blush on her cheeks. She glanced at him from time to time with her beautiful emerald green eyes that were almost too large for her face. He couldn't believe that after everything he had to go through to get her, she was finally here with him. She embodied everything he could have hoped. When he saw her, he saw pieces of himself intensified. She was faultless.

He heard her giggle as he poured her Mr. Bubbles into the warm bathwater. She began to play with her Barbie mermaids as he took out her bath towel. He dipped it in the water and began to wipe her face and back. She stuck out her hand as he scrubbed every finger individually. He began to wash her shoulders, then drifted toward her torso. Her beautiful porcelain skin glistened. He touched her legs delicately, rubbing the cloth along the smooth insides enough to make sure he got every spot. He lingered in that area; her skin felt incredible. He slid his hand up and slipped it in and out of her warm frame skillfully. He knew she would enjoy him washing her everywhere as much as he did. Anyone would, but he couldn't understand why she wouldn't look in his eyes. He even grabbed her chin and forced her to face him, but she closed her eyes to avoid the contact. She never spoke.

When Ruby woke up she quickly got dressed and made her bed. She tucked in each corner neatly. She knew her father would check for "military corners" later. She left her room to eat breakfast. Her father was already making her favorite—corn fritters. She ate quickly so that she could return to her room to "read," as she told him every Saturday morning. Once she was done she picked up her book and went to her bed to sit down. During the night her teddy bear had fallen to the floor. She picked her up, held her in her hands, and asked if she should do what she wanted to. She seemed reassured by Teddy's response. Teddy saw her and her father in the bathroom the first time, and Ruby knew Teddy stayed awake with her every night that he came into her room. Teddy and she knew this was the most pivotal point in her life. Today would decide if she took control of her life. Today would be her ultimate trial.

Ruby quietly went to her closet; he might have been listening. She pulled out her step stool and stretched up just far enough to pull down her old Halloween costume. She had hidden some of the pills the doctor had given her in its pockets. Originally, her mother had given her father the pills so that he could administer them every night Ruby spent at his house. But since he refused to give Ruby her pills, the doctor and her mother decided to discontinue the medication, as it might be detrimental to not consistently take it. Yet now, they decided that Ruby was old enough to take the pills by herself. Before the doctor decided, she had had a long conversation with Ruby. Her mom and the doctor explained that it was essential to keep this a secret, just between them. Ruby knew what that meant. She had overheard them in the halls discussing whether Ruby getting her medicine was worth the risk of her father finding out she was sneaking it.

"What will these pills do?" asked her mother. The doctor explained, "Paxil is safe to use in children. I have seen many children succeed when using Paxil. It will decrease her anxiety, lift her out of her depression, and negate some of the effects of her post-traumatic stress disorder. Hopefully she won't be such a handful at home."

"What if he catches her? How will he punish her?"

"I don't think we can know. We can work to prepare her and figure out how to hide them. If we don't do this now she may not be able to survive. We are going to have to think about the benefits. Have you been able to stop her thumb sucking?"

"No, but now she only sucks at night."

"At eight a child should not be sucking her thumb. Last time we talked, we agreed that if her stress level was so high that she can't stop thumb sucking, it was necessary to start her on some medications."

"I know you're right. Let's go ahead and try it. I know she is under immense stress. I think the medication started to have an effect before we stopped it the last time."

The doctor began to ask her mother about the custody trial again. The doctor sighed loudly when her mother said nothing was being done, despite the doctor's testimony. The courts did not want to alienate any fathers. The visitation on Wednesdays and every other weekend was part of the movement for protecting "fathers' rights."

When they had returned to the room, they explained to Ruby that following the directions was very important because taking too many of the pills could kill her. They made her promise to never do that on purpose. They "contracted for safety," as the doctor put it. Ruby didn't really understand how taking a little white pill could make her not fear and despise her father, but she decided her mom and the doctor might know what was better for her than she did.

Her mom had aided Ruby in smuggling in the pills. She sewed special pockets into shirts because Ruby's father went through everything she brought into the house except what she was wearing. Her mom helped her plan where she should hide them. They decided it was best to keep only one or two in each area in case he found them. If they didn't put the pills in a bottle and stored only a few in secret spots, he might overlook them, thinking they were lint or bits of mint Lifesavers. For extra safety, Ruby had rotated hiding spots.

That afternoon, Ruby went into her sock drawer and pulled out her special Easter Bunny socks. She kept two in there. She looked at her stuffed animal rack and pulled out Kaleidoscope, the multi-print cat, from her beanie babies. There was a little tear in which she had hidden three pills. She gathered them all into a little pile and went out to watch TV. For dinner she requested mashed potatoes.

After dinner she cleared the table and her father went to pick out a show "they could both enjoy." That usually meant the news or the Duke basketball game. Today she pretended to watch instead of bringing her American girl doll out to play with as usual. Her father fell asleep, beer within arm's reach. She quietly, slowly sneaked off to her room. She took the pills and brought them into the TV room. She dropped each one individually into the beer. She watched as each pill fizzed when it hit the drink. With the last two she had to stir the can a little to get them to dissolve fully. She knew her father would never let a drop of beer go to waste, even if it tasted funny. The beer had only a couple of sips left.

She went into her room and found her dog leash. She slipped out the back door and unleashed the dog that her father always kept outside. That dog was alone every day and night. When the dog came inside the house her father would beat it, even if he invited her in. He always said he was "training" her. Ruby didn't particularly care for the dog; she just thought it was cruel to leave her there.

They headed to the park. Sitting on the swings, Ruby expected someone to see her and call the cops when she refused to talk. She thought they would take her to her father's house, and when, hopefully, he didn't answer the door, they would enter, only to find his body. If he had only been hurt, she thought he would never want to see her again. If he died, she knew no one would press charges against an eight-year-old. She would never go on trial. It was clear that the court system had really committed the crime. It had ignored her pleas to not be left alone with her father. At least her mother and the doctor believed her. She realized they had been right; the pills *did* help her live without anxiety.

Twelve

by Peter Wien

They stand with their backs against the walls.
Loosely draped and hungry they watch
as the food of their lust walks by.

Voices are rarely used here. Mainly the eyes talk.
And the dim, smoky light hides well their truth.
The stench of overworked and abused bodies
fills an air permeated with the incense of drugs.
While off the halls, in shoddy rooms, behind loosely fit doors
they come together, on overused mattresses
amid the risk of pestilence and disease
to seek fulfillment in a most unfulfilling way,
while the specter of the death's head hangs above each bed
and slowly erodes the trilogy of their being.

For here, in this lonely wasteland of human flesh,
each encounter becomes one more nail of crucifixion
to lives already devoid of hope
and crumbling beneath the weight of their own crosses.
It is a place where men seeking the excitement of life,
in their desperate loneliness actually come to die unto themselves.

In this darkness a young boy walks confused, alone, afraid.
His child's body does not yet reflect its past years of abuse.
He is a prize here, a plum, a highly sought after object.

In this place, to these men, he is seen as many things...
but no one sees him as human.

He has come here, this child, into the slums, voluntarily,
from a fine uptown hotel, where every comfort is freely supplied.
As he walks with his own wary and hungry eye,
stalking the stalkers, he recalls the toy plane his mother
had bought him earlier that day, in another
time, in another place, in another world.

His pulse quickens and his slight body shakes, as he sidesteps
the grasp of a towel-clad man, sitting with a group at a broken table,
cooking heroin in the top of a bottle cap.

He pauses as the horror of realization begins to wedge itself
into his already raped and polluted young mind.
His eyes begin to rapidly search for a point of safety
as he realizes that he left safety somewhere far behind.
Suddenly, in his darkness, a body, a face, strange but somewhat easy
reaches out and speaks a kind and gentle word.
A hand touches and moves slowly across his barren flesh.
It seems to understand.

Slowly and gently it begins to pull him away.
A door closes behind them, and he tries to talk.
But soon the talk fades as experienced and hungry hands
move quickly and with greed to their desire.
He closes his eyes and is pulled down to the bed of death.
Soon it will all be over.

It is here that the passions of an emerging youth become twisted
as the search for life in this confusion becomes lust

and the spilled and wasted seeds rot on a stinking mattress
along with a lost innocence.

A boy's body being driven through sensations
of a manhood still years from emergence.
A boy's mind being pulled and twisted and formed
by the teachers of death.
A boy's spirit being beaten and trampled
in the land of degradation.
A boy's heart being torn and eaten by the jackals
of his own confused being as the light of his soul
slowly begins to dim.

Eventually the passions of the body begin to firm their grasp
as a vial passes below his nostrils and the thoughts of hope
and pain vanish into the desire of a purely physical flesh,
along with the false promise of escape everlasting.

And so they are done, this stranger and he.
Now the familiar idle conversation
begins to build the bridge for polite escape.

Soon he is closing the door behind him,
pulling the towel tight around his waist.
He walks to the shower,
not wanting to look into the laughing vultures' eyes,
praying no one will touch him.
He scrubs his body, but cannot come clean.
Around him some are playfully talking and joking
while others, like him, try to hide in their vulnerability of this new light.
Time here, devoid of hunger, seems to last forever.

Soon, but not soon enough, he is clothed and making his way
to a broken red exit light, over a secured door, that marks his escape.
He breaks through the door, trying to conceal his intense desire to run.

The doors open and he descends the long brownstone steps
into the predawn of the city.
The air here smells strangely sweet by comparison.
And yet on the sidewalk below he sees the drunken bodies
of yet other broken men lying littered among the shattered bottles
of cheap city wine.

As he reaches the walk, and stands among the refuse, he looks back.
A plaque tells him that this was once the home of James Fenimore
    Cooper.
His stomach knots; he wants to vomit.
It makes him think of school and little Donna Winslow
Who still too sucks her thumb.
It is a secret that they share, but from afar.
For he has a secret that will not entitle him to come any closer.

And so he begins the very long walk uptown to respectability,
while singing songs of romance and love and hope
that seem somehow strangely lost to him.
He walks in a world he does not really feel part of.

Finally back in his room he begins to slowly undress.
He looks at his naked reflection in the mirror and turns to his bed
and to the toy plane quietly waiting by the window.

As he pulls back the covers, he remembers the man's words.
"You don't belong here. Go home. One day, you will make beautiful
    babies."

That is what the man had said, but only after he had had his way with
   him.

He begins to pray to God for deliverance, and as always
an anesthetic cloud begins to form in the region of his mind
where memories are stored. Soon their pain becomes so dulled
it is as if they are forgotten or had never happened.

Soon, he can hear his mother speaking with his father in the adjoining
   room.
She is requesting a favor for him, a favor that the "boy" had wanted so
   much
the day before. It all seems meaningless to him now.
But he knows, as the memories of the night begin to fade, another lie
   begins.
Another lie until the hunger cries out again.

To him the world seemed full of lies. Life was lies. Love was lies, God
   was lies.
He wondered if death was lies, too.

The Night to Remember

by Ahn Pearl

It was supposed to be a night to celebrate
a night of happiness and joy
a night in honor of finishing a long struggle.

It starts out that way: happy laughter, friendly conversation.
Then I see him, the handsome man that I know from work.
We talk for the first time that night, exchange numbers and flirtatious
    words.

I go and meet him, alone, but happy that I have made a friend.
I am not afraid because I know him and his kindness.
He touches me as we walk, and I feel safe and warm, cared for.

Then we kiss. I am happy. I like him and it feels good to know that he
    feels the same.
We go back to his place and begin to undress.
I feel a little overwhelmed but do not say anything.
I want to be with him. I want him to touch me.

Things suddenly change. My body is in pain. His voice changes.
The kindness is gone and coldness takes over. Only his needs matter now.
I don't want this. I want to leave. Small parts of me start to die.
I am afraid to talk, to speak up; inside I am screaming for this to stop.

Will he hurt me more? I am alone. I am isolated.

The pain becomes too much, and I start to scream and cry; my mouth
    is covered.
His hands are over my mouth. They silence me. I endure the pain.
I don't know what is happening. I am alone, wondering when it will
    end,
willing to do anything for it to end. I need to get out; I need to leave.

He exits my body and then kneels over me. He has not finished.
His cold words fill the air again. I comply with his request,
fearful of what will happen if I do not.
I am curled on his bed, lying in fear, waiting for it to be over.

I feel his hot liquid on my face and neck.
It is over, I have satisfied him.
I can go now. I am still alive.

I leave quickly. Walking quickly, I look back once and see my rapist
    blocks behind me.
I shower at home, the water hot and fast,
washing away evidence, washing away the rape.

I dry off and cry. I hold my body.
My body is in pain. My insides burn.
There is a fire between my legs. There is an anger inside me.

My body still hurts the next day. My mind races.
His face pops into my head, his voice fills my ears,
the handsome man that I work with.

A night to remember.
A memory for all the wrong reasons.

Awakening

by Susan S. Russell, M.A.

Awakening: swollen eyelids opening to blurred vision. Through this blurred vision I see tree branches far above me. I am lying under the canopy of a deep, dark forest. My head feels foggy, my thoughts unclear. Where am I? What am I doing here? Intense pain begins to emanate from my head. I slowly lift my hand and touch my head. I feel something sticky, and what feels like a bird's nest, but in reality my fingers are intertwining in my hair. As I begin to grope about my head more and more, I feel something sharp and protruding. The rest of my body begins to awaken and starts to shake uncontrollably. Even though summer has just begun I feel cold as if an ice storm has invaded my entire body. I reach out again, touching my body, and I realize I am naked. Slowly my eyesight becomes more focused. My thoughts and memory of what has happened hit me like a tidal wave. I've been raped, beaten, and left here in these woods. Tears begin to fall like a hard rain while at the same time my hand reaches out, groping around for my clothes, anything to stop the cold shivers that rack my body. However, I find only one piece of clothing, and I am not sure what it is nor if it is enough to cover up my body.

Still clutching this material I try to sit up, but the intense sharp pain in my head makes this almost impossible. I sit still, not moving, trying to make the pain subside, as the realization of my situation begins to surface. As a trained emergency medical technician, I am aware of the grave position I am in. I need medical attention, and I need it right away. My eyes feel very swollen and even when I do look around it is dark. After what seems like eternity, I manage to stand and begin to stumble around. Next thing I know, I am standing in front of a tent. In a shaky voice I cry out, "Help me, please help me, I've been raped." After a moment I see a youth stick his head out of the tent. The look of shock registers immediately on his face as I stand there trying to cover up my body using the material I have in my hands. He quickly scrambles out as others are stirring in the tent. He pokes his head back in the tent, whispers something, and brings out some type of clothing. He helps me put it on. By now all the others are out of the tent, among them a young girl who begins to give directions. The first youth then helps me into the tent and into a warm sleeping bag. I begin mumbling, calling out for my husband. In the background the youths discuss their plan of action. Soon waves of nausea begin to flood me, and I struggle to move, knowing I am going to be sick. The youth who had remained in vigilant watch over me helps me to the entrance of the tent and I begin to vomit uncontrollably. Just as the ambulance arrives, I hear the sound of birds chirping, announcing the coming of dawn.

ATTACK FOLLOWS STOP FOR FLAT TIRE

It all began on June 19, 1992, while driving down the road in a 1977 Ford Thunderbird late at night. I realized I had a flat tire. I pulled into a well-lit inn's parking lot under a giant maple tree to examine it further. I knew that changing a flat on this big rig would be difficult, if not impossible, for me. Soon a man I had met only briefly earlier that night and who had made a derogatory comment to me pulled in alongside my car. He offered to give me a ride. At first I refused. I wanted to use the inn's telephone and call home, but then as I looked around, I saw that the inn had closed for the night and everything appeared locked up tight.

At the time, innocence, ignorance, and faith in people, even those who make derogatory comments, were attributes of mine. After all, I lived in a small town nestled in the Green Mountains, where everyone knew just about everyone. I thought of crime as limited to small-time burglaries. I decided to accept this ride and grabbed my things. Little did I know that the moment I closed the car door,

I would lose everything, all the material possessions, my innocence, my trust in mankind, my physical stamina, my emotional stability, EVERYTHING. Later I would learn that during the initial investigation it was discovered that two of my car tires had been slashed. This information helped me to realize that my offender had intended to kidnap me, whether I had agreed to go willingly or not.

INVESTIGATION AND TREATMENT BECOME PART OF THE TRAUMA

Upon arrival at a near-by local hospital—to stabilize my injuries and prepare me for transportation to another hospital that specialized in severe trauma—I recall a young detective entering the emergency room. He introduced himself, told me that my husband was being contacted, and apologized, saying, "I'm so sorry this has happened to you. However, we would like to catch whoever did this to you, so I'd like to ask you a few questions." Although at the time I recall feeling intense pain, dazed, confused, and scared, I was able to provide the detective with a brief summary of events leading up to the current time, a description of the man who had kidnapped, raped, and beaten me, and a depiction of the car he was driving.

During this initial interview, the doctor began to conduct a rape exam. I recall the detective informing me that he would be stepping out of the room momentarily while the doctor performed some of the tasks associated with a rape exam. This exam is one that is forever ingrained in my mind; I still remember being strapped to the backboard—severely injured and once again feeling a lack of control—while a male performed intrusive measures on me.

Transported to a second hospital, one that specialized in severe trauma, I remember the nurses and doctors there had a way of treating you in a much more caring and supportive way than in the first hospital. And although I was surrounded by medical professionals and my husband, I felt the intense fear of knowing that the man still roamed around and would most likely seek me out to finish the job he thought he had done, that of killing me. The hospital working with the police decided to hide my true identity and change my name. This in itself offered some comfort, but made it difficult for friends and caring individuals to locate me.

EXPERIENCE WITH CRIMINAL JUSTICE SYSTEM BRINGS MORE TRAUMA

In less than a week, the police had caught this man. Though relieved, I feared the legal road ahead, that of having to face this man again in court. However, since I had never been involved in legal proceedings such as this, I did not realize the tribulations I would face in dealing with prosecutors and defense lawyers. There are specifically two circumstances that are vividly etched in my mind when experiencing the criminal justice system. They are a grueling deposition and the final hearing in which I had to face my attacker.

One of the first difficult challenges in the criminal justice system I had to endure was the deposition. I shall never forget the horrifying experience of being questioned by my attacker's attorney. He asked some very personal, in-depth, explicit sexual questions to which I, under oath, had to provide the answers. The victim's advocate—after seeing me burst into tears and be unable to control the flow of these tears—eventually persuaded the defense lawyer to curb his questioning. Feeling totally humiliated by this process is an understatement. By the time the deposition was over, I felt I was standing completely naked before the enemy. I felt stripped of everything including my dignity, which at that point was shaky at best.

The second and perhaps the biggest and most difficult challenge that I had to complete came the day I walked into that courtroom and faced my attacker. On one side of the room sat newspaper and television reporters, with their cameras and pens rolling. Present also in the courtroom were people who supported me, members of my community, people who worked on my case, my attacker's family, and security. *Not wanting my attacker to see my eyes, I wore sunglasses.* To feel safe, I surrounded myself with family members and good friends, took a deep breath, and entered this room. My attacker sat in shackles and chains at the defense table 20 feet in front of me. After listening to testimony from prosecution and defense witnesses, it was my turn. I remember how my hand shook uncontrollably as I held it up to swear I would tell the whole truth and nothing but the truth, so help me God. After answering the prosecutor and defense attorney's questions, I read a powerful and moving statement that I had written concerning the effects that this traumatic event had on my life. A brief excerpt is as follows:

> I feel very terrified to be in the presence of a man who almost killed me and stole from me so many things that were important to me. There have been many days when I thought the only way to survive would be to join the spirit world. I've contemplated suicide many times as a means to escape the torture and suffering I've been through and will have to go through the rest of my life due to this person. He values no one's life. He does not care about life.
>
> I remember waking up in the hospital in so much pain, I really thought that if I had died it would not have hurt as much. The days and months after were filled with physical and emotional pain. People such as doctors, investigators, friends, and family say I am lucky to be alive; some days I wonder about that.
>
> What is a good night's sleep? I don't know anymore. If I could be a bear, I could hibernate for many winters with the lost amount of sleep. Nightmares: the scariest, most terrifying movie couldn't come close to matching these personal horrifying nightmares.
>
> My everyday concerns are with trying to comprehend what happened to me, trying to comprehend the legal system. I am trying to deal with my right to privacy—my life invaded by the media.
>
> An additional hardship has been dealing with all the financial burden I have now, because my offender got out of control. The medical expenses alone even with insurance and victim's compensation are astronomical.
>
> I do not have the words to describe what this has done to my husband's and my future or the dreams we had. (Russell 4/93)

CHALLENGE OF OFFENDER'S RELEASE STILL TO COME

Sitting in front of the courtroom and the people in attendance, and facing my attacker, was by far the hardest challenge that I had to face since surviving the attack.

However, now, almost a decade later, after having survived the experience of working with the criminal justice system to see my offender caught, tried, and sentenced, I will be faced with yet another challenge, one which at the moment seems the most difficult to face: the reality of my offender's release. This, however, is another chapter in my life, another story to write and to share with readers at another time.

The Reporter: The Whole Story

I had just finished reading a poem about sexual violence to the House Judicial Committee, at the statehouse in Montpelier, Vermont, when I was introduced to the reporter. He was writing a story about sex offender treatment and wanted to talk to "a survivor." I agreed to an interview, and we went to sit in an elegant room that was darkly and sparsely furnished. He began by asking me what I thought about the effectiveness of treatment for sex offenders. I responded, "Well, I haven't looked at the research and recidivism rates, so I can't tell you much about its effectiveness." So he changed tact. He simply wanted to talk to someone who had experienced sexual violence, collecting information to add to his story. My expertise was solid on this point and that was apparently enough.

He wanted to know if there had been too much emphasis on sex offender treatment during the firestorm that was ignited when a Vermont judge sentenced a man who had pleaded guilty to repeatedly sexually assaulting a girl from the ages of six to ten to a 60-day prison sentence. "No, I don't. I just think that prevention needs as much or more attention." We talked a bit more about this before he said, "About your situation. Would you mind telling me about your situation?" I looked him straight in the eye and said, "I don't want to talk about the details within this context." This is not for public consumption, I thought to myself.

I was reminded again about what people want to know and simultaneously deny or don't want to know. Many people seem to have a voracious appetite for the details of such stories in a global, Jerry Springer–Oprah talk-show sort of way. But while the specifics of the abuse are important for me to share with select people in my life, those aren't the details that I think educate the public about sexual violence. What is instructive about my story is the sequel, what happened next. What I've learned about survival, compassion, and spiritual development. How I have come to realize that while my childhood was about being small in order to survive, my adult years have been about getting bigger, becoming whole, in order to live fully.

I begin to feel as if I am being asked to fit 25 years of knowledge, suffering, and healing onto the head of a pin. Dance for me, little girl. "I could kill you and no-one would know." "You're hands are lovely, just like your mother's." But I'm afraid of strange men. Will this one hurt me, too? "But where was your mother? Did your mother know?" Yes. No. Maybe. Always. These are all truths. You can line them up, make a crossword puzzle out of them, or a collage, or maybe an Andy Warhol–style print. The latter would be as interesting as a Campbell's soup can, especially with the title, *"Did her mother know he was fucking her?"* Or you could ask my mother yourself. Go to her house, sit on her couch, and listen to her talk and talk and talk and talk. She could tell you about her volunteer pursuits ad nauseum. Then she'd work backward: she was a small business owner (day care, furniture store) and a teacher for 30-plus years before this. At 76, she volunteers her remaining life away. She walks into the statehouse as an activist, too, for the protection and improvement of teacher retirement benefits. I asked her if she was going to the statehouse, on the same day I was scheduled to be there, in order to prepare myself should our paths have crossed. I imagined our interaction: "Why are you here?" "Didn't you hear? Your violent, crazy partner of 11 years molested me."

Did your mother know? Does she know now? I think her hearing is still failing her on this point. "I'm afraid I will learn something that will haunt me the rest of my life. Do you know what I mean?" she said to me when I confronted her several years ago. Tell me about it. For years it silenced me, as if his penis was permanently lodged in my throat. But no longer. Now I am not only big, but I have a voice. I don't shake anymore when I talk about this and I understand what can be gained from transforming the personal experience of violence into something meaningful beyond my life.

The reporter looked at me and said, "It must have taken some work to get to this place. You seem so—okay about it." Little sirens start faintly screeching inside me. "Yes," is all I can bring myself to say firmly. Twice. "Yes." Then later to myself,

I think: Yes, I'm fine about it. Jim Dandy. No, that wasn't his name, but did I tell you he was well mannered, articulate, handsome, a middle-to-upper-middle-class businessman who wore three-piece suits and had a taste for collecting antiques and coins? Yes, I'm okay about it. You mean because I'm articulate and dress nicely? Because I'm here, dammit? No, I will never be okay about it. It will never be okay. But that's a helluva lot different than being tanked or cowed by it, shame flaming in my face, terror shaking my limbs.

But you gotta know this, too. The part I didn't tell you. All those words that could have streamed out behind the "Yes." I will probably always have surprising moments when all of a sudden the animal part of me just freaks, the reptilian brain as Peter Levine refers to it in his book, *Waking the Tiger,* on healing trauma. One moment, normal life, fullsteam ahead; the next, my brain is screaming *F-L-I-G-H-T !* Like when a bald doctor got his head too close to mine, and I smelled his scalp oil, saw the gleaming, bare skin, and felt like a 50-pound weight had dropped directly on my lungs, breathlessness taking me to the edge for a split second. And then... Yeah, I'm okay. Yeah, really, I'm okay.

Yes. No. Maybe. Always. These are all truths.

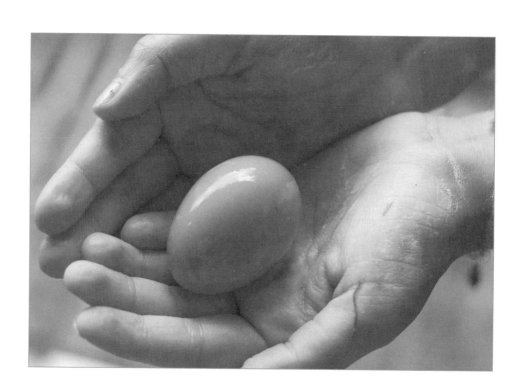

My Wounded Warrior

by Dale Coleman

There's a little boy in me
He's hiding deep
in the darkest corners
of my soul

He is afraid
but not of this dark place
He is afraid
of the light outside

He feels safe
in this dark place
It is warm and no one
can see him there

He can cry and
feel the pain
and no one will laugh
and no one will tease
because he does this all
in the safety and quiet of
his dark place

I think that he's been trying
to venture out of the dark place
but he is afraid

and he is unsure
because in the light
all of his feelings and emotions
are confused

Outside the dark place
in the light
everything feels like
sadness
and many things
make him feel afraid
so he retreats

I tell him, it's okay
come out now
I will stand by you,
protect you
and let you feel.
Out here in the light
we can feel together

Yet he does not trust me
He has felt alone so long
He is my abandoned self
My neglected child
who feels forgotten
and who cannot forget
my shame

But I know the truth
about this courageous boy
He does not deserve

to live in darkness
feeling the shame
the pain
and the guilt

For it is to him
I owe my life,
my very survival
I am waiting here
to welcome him
and care for him
I know now who he is
he is my Wounded Warrior

The Rape

by Kitty Garn

I don't think I've ever written this down. I've tried to write it down, but it never flowed like it usually flows when I write. But I've been telling the story for years, because I've found a lot of people out there who actually needed to hear it, since the same thing happened to them in one manner or another. I've always been completely open about this part of my past, but I think a lot of that, especially in the early years, was about trying to get it off me somehow.

When I was sixteen, the rest of my gang was fifteen. I was the only one who could drive. We'd get someone to buy us alcohol, and we would drive around looking for a party. I actually learned to drive while I was drunk since I was the only one who could, and I wasn't going to miss out on all the fun.

We started at a party with private-school seniors. I drank a quart of Bacardi and a half a quart of Bacardi mixed with beer. I was feeling no pain, and, up until that night of my life, had never been inclined to feel any fear. We got wind of another party at the estate of the most popular boy in my school, only it wasn't him that was throwing it; it was his older brother who was home from college.

I can remember the beginning. I walked in with my two friends, and for some reason we were the only girls there. I remember feeling comfortable in the living room next to a gigantic fireplace. Someone decided it was time to do shots, and I challenged a guy to a contest. I had two more double shots of Bacardi.

I have no recollection of anything after that.

I woke up the next morning on the floor of a bedroom with my skirt off and puke all over my shirt. I looked up at a bed and, I'll never forget this, saw the long, sculpted arm of the guy that every girl in town wanted to date. I knew someone had had sex with me because I wasn't a virgin; only difference this time was I could barely walk. I remember thinking, "Who wants to have sex with a girl who has puke on her shirt?" I went to sneak out and go home and found that my car was gone. I picked up the phone, steadying myself, because I was still stinking drunk, and called my "friends."

"Yeah, we took your car. Didn't know what else to do. Guess you're going to have to get a ride."

I walked down the hallway into some TV room where several guys were already awake. I had no idea if I had had sex with the guy in the bedroom, or with one of the guys in front of me, or with all of them. There was one guy with a kind face, and I asked him if he could take me to my friend's house. That was a mighty long drive. He had some vintage Camaro and wouldn't shut up about it. I was trying desperately not to puke in his car.

A few months later, I ran into the guy to whom I had given my virginity. He was actually always very sweet to me. He was there that night, even though I don't remember seeing him. He told me that I had stopped breathing, and they had dragged me to the bathtub for a cold shower, but by the time they got me in it, I had started breathing and puking so they figured I was going to be okay. It was at that moment that my 15-year-old friends decided to take my car and leave me alone in a house with at least five guys.

For the next seven years, I thought of that night as the night I got drunk, blacked out, and had sex with one or many guys. I thought, "You were drunk and you got fucked." It never occurred to me that I was raped, because I viewed rape as something that happens to people who have the opportunity to fight back, aren't drunk, and haven't been promiscuous before. It was like I thought I had it coming. I never should have lost my always present composure. I shouldn't have been that drunk.

And wouldn't you know, I haven't been that drunk again? I've easily consumed that much alcohol and more, but that is the only time in my entire life that I have EVER blacked out. I've spent the last 20 years drinking more than every man in the room and still standing because I will forever be the last to close my eyes.

When I was 23, right before my first marriage, I read an article about gang rape. It listed the behavioral patterns of women or girls, as in my case, after they have been gang raped. It was like reading the story of my own life, and from then on, I started classifying what had happened to me as rape.

Seven years is a long time to go without getting any help or closure for what had happened to me. During that time, I tried to kill myself four times.

The first attempt landed me in the hospital and the last, around the age of 21, left me with scars on my wrists from hitting an artery. I dated abusive men who were always older and perfectly content to treat me like the piece of trash I thought I was. I was desperate for their attention and the meaner they were to me, the better I felt. I looked to them to confirm the agonizing sense of worthlessness I could not escape. I drank alcohol every chance I got, even if it meant getting a six-pack and driving around in the country, so my parents wouldn't know.

Nobody knew what was wrong with me because I didn't know what was wrong with myself. I just sank into the role of the good-hearted, disturbed kid that some parents get saddled with and wish they could just lock away in the attic.

Of course, I still over-achieved. I went to college at 17, performed in numerous plays and musicals, and was always the life of the party. I traveled all over the country as a horseback-riding instructor, including a stint as head coach of a university equestrian team.

By the time I hit 30, I could actually feel safe sleeping in a house by myself. Sleep and any form of letting go has always been a tall order for me, since that night, because very bad things can happen to people who sleep or let go or are unconscious and nearly dead. I'm still not a huge fan of darkness, and I battle every day to feel worthy, especially in a relationship.

The thing I know about rape is that it took away who I might have been and left me with a person who will always have to wonder. I always say how much I would have loved the chance to tell that girl good-bye and that I loved her because she died that night, and I can't ever see her, feel her, again. I'm still learning how to love myself, to not be desperate to please and prove my worth to people.

The tendency to blame the victim runs rampant with rape, but you know, I've never heard someone say to a person who just got robbed, "So why did you have such nice things?" People have choices to make every day and those bastards made the wrong fucking choice. When I hear about people getting raped or molested and surviving, I've always thought that in some ways they might have been better off dead. Don't get me wrong, I am soooooo glad to be alive, but it comes with the knowledge that the other me, the one who could have made love fearlessly, looked people in the eye, and trusted people who deserved it instead of the ones who didn't, would have been as spectacular on the inside as people thought she was on the outside.

I guess there's a reason I never wrote this story down. It still makes me sick.

Carved in Stone

by Jon

Maybe I'll wear this secret like a
second skin, coat myself in gray paint,
suffocate,
smear gray on everything I touch,
breathe gray air,
eat gray food,
move through a gray world,
sleep in a gray bed,
have a gray job,
pray to a gray God.
      Maybe I'll paint gray pictures on gray canvases,
sing gray songs to gray people
who sit in gray church pews.
      Maybe I'll try to turn my wife gray,
bathe my children in gray water,
stop for gray red lights,
see gray movies,
eat the gray flesh of ten-thousand gray cows,
      or Maybe,
I'll scrub myself with 1,000 pounds of sand,
      roll in it, grind it onto every
      square inch of my gray skin
      until I stand,
Fresh
Blazing
Red and white and pink and black, exfoliated, under

a boiling yellow sun, see
every color of the visible spectrum
and stop apologizing. Given enough time,
even glaciers melt.

Stone may crumble to gray dust,
but dust dissolves into colorless atoms.

The Road Back

by Marcia

I didn't believe in love. Plain and simple. I didn't believe in God and I trusted no one. Really, how could I? That place in me was all dammed up—loss upon loss, disappointment upon disappointment. I looked to no one for help and at an early age devised a safety plan that was contingent upon these concepts: trust no one, feel nothing, perfect a false self to be presented to the world, fool everyone. I believed in these concepts. They worked so well I fooled myself and, ultimately, lost myself.

And yet somehow I was a fighter. Always. Somehow I had a shred of dignity that forced me to fight for my life. This is what saved me.

And this is what almost killed me. When I was seven my grandfather raped me. I remember much of it, his face over mine, the room, the bed. But mostly his face over mine. And my confusion. At first it seems like maybe fun, something new. Then it turns to confusion—what is this? Is this okay? Why does my body feel this way? What is this? Why is he looking at me this way? I don't know what it means. What is this feeling in my body: is it good or bad? What is happening? And then. Now I know it's bad. My mother is suddenly here, I can see her face, feel the rage, the hot, burning rage. The hatred. And the pain.

She is enraged at me. She drags me down the hallway by my hair—it hurts so. I put my hand between hers and my head to try to stop the pain. What is happening, what is happening? Now I'm in the bathroom and she is hitting me and saying bad things.

And then it is still. She turns off the light and closes the door. I am in the dark. My head is near the toilet, I can smell it. My body feels broken. It's dark. I can barely breathe. I am terrified. The toilet smells; the tiles are cold; I am hot and I'm not crying. I can't. I am too still, too frozen.

How did I get up? I was so little. How did I find my way off the bathroom floor? Where did that strength come from? Why didn't I remain on the floor and wait for help? My life as I knew it was over; the world had suddenly become a very different place, and I was absolutely alone and broken. Sometimes when I recall the heroic act of getting off the floor, I feel so proud of myself, and I try to harness that deep strength to help me in difficult situations. But the road from the bathroom floor to the pride was very difficult, very long, and very painful.

The memory of the assault remained buried for many years and then it emerged, bit by agonizing bit. Much of the work I did in psychotherapy was to clear away the heavy debris that had been shielding me from remembering this horror.

Before, life could not have been too good but it was the life I knew. I was a child before, and in many ways I led the life that was expected of a Jewish, middle-class child. I was innocent and enthusiastic about life. I was part of a fairly large extended family, doing the things a little girl does. I must have experienced my mother and grandfather's rage before but I imagine I found ways of making it okay, the way children do. I don't think I knew about shame then. Afterward, my life was drenched in shame, which oozed into every cell, every crevice, every thought, every word. I could escape it only by leaving myself; I had no choice.

After, the world was a very dangerous place, and I alone was responsible for my survival. After, there was no one else in my world. I couldn't see anyone else. I could only make people up and try to bend them to my will.

And yet I fought. At a deep, often unconscious level, I knew this feeling was wrong. I knew that I deserved a life. Later, I realized I had been desperately searching for the child I had left on the bathroom floor. I wanted to find her but didn't know how. Her calls to me went unheeded; I couldn't hear them. The longer I ignored her, the more I acted out. I lied. I cheated. I stole. She drove my anger and my recovery; she somehow showed me the way back. This wonderful, loving, believing child never gave up hope.

And now, I do believe but I struggle with this belief. There is still a part of me that feels certain that safety is found in isolation. But year by year, the struggle is lessened and my heart is fuller. This struggle gave me my life back. Without it my sense of self would have stayed on the bathroom floor. I had to dismantle the constructs, one by one, to get to the disappointment and the loss.

I was first able to see the child when I was in my 30s. She appeared in a series of dreams, and she in fact led me to the incest memory. I had been in therapy for over 15 years when I began to get a strong sense of my inner child. I remember my therapist asking if I wanted to have him hold my inner child for me until I was ready. This touched my heart; we both knew she was there, close by, waiting to be found.

My husband helped me reach her. When my husband and I first met, we had an immediate heart connection; our inner children recognized kindred spirits and immediately bonded. It would be many years before we would be able to live as fully functioning adults; we are still works-in-progress, and I am glad of that. Year after year, we work side by side on our individual recoveries, mindful of nurturing our relationship and encouraging each other's growth.

In a similar way, as my sister and I grew older, we found a place where we could mutually love and respect each other. My first internalized, maternal voice was an echo of her adult voice nurturing me; our recovered relationship has also taken years of healing as individuals.

I also have learned how to be a friend, to be present, attentive, and loving. One very dear friend, in particular, saw something in me and taught me, ever so patiently, the joys of friendship.

And the wonder of my life—my own biological child is now 20 years old. Until I was in my 30s, I had no desire to be a mother. And then something moved. As the ice over my heart melted, I suddenly and spontaneously began visualizing a child running up and down the hallway of our home. What an incredible gift he is. How he has enriched my life and deepened my recovery. The child inside me adores my son. In many ways, they grew up together. That I turned out to be a good enough mother is a testament to human spirit.

And somehow, after years of rigid atheism, I have become an ardent believer. This still amazes me. I believe in love, I trust others, and I believe in God. Odd for one like me but true. This faith has changed my life in ways previously unimaginable. I often feel contained, feel as if God is leading me so I can finally let go. I also struggle with this idea; it is an uphill battle. I see people more clearly. I am kinder, warmer, and I often feel as if I actually am part of a larger whole; I often want to belong.

My spiritual belief has given me the ability to forgive those who have hurt me, especially my mother. I have empathy for her, for her life of rage, lack of fulfillment, and loneliness. I can feel how awful it must have been for her to have hated her own child, to have never known love. I will never trust her but this is okay. Somehow we have built something of a relationship. It doesn't look like other mother–daughter relationships, it has no foundation but is based on what we've been able to cobble together in the last few years—it is something, after years of nothing.

I have become fairly disciplined, and I have morning and evening rituals that help me to feel safe and connected. In the evening, my husband and I share a spiritual reading and tell each other what we were grateful for during the day, and what we hope to find the willingness to do the following day. In the morning, I say a short prayer before I get out of bed, then meditate and write in my journal. Each morning's entry ends in exactly the same way: My joy is in the center of my body, the place between the front and the back. This is where the child lives. She is precious; alive, engaged, and connected. Sometimes she is sad, angry, lonely, anguished, but she is always alive—that is the joy. I pray for the willingness to stay connected to this splendor; thank you for leading me here.

The Abyss

by Linda Schritt

The black tide of memory rolls over me.
The fragile illusion of my life disappearing into its swell

And I fall from any grace I thought was mine
into a deep abyss of dark despair.

Where fear and desolation twist inside me
until my body sweats with the effort to constrain it.

I am held hostage there by my own
dread of what I will find if I look too close.

I hold my hands up to my face
and cover my eyes

Hoping like the child I once was that if I can no longer see
I will have somehow become invisible.

For I would deny the pain of my existence
and choose instead to live inside a place of nothingness

Where joy can no longer reach me
but neither can despair.

But a small voice whispers in the darkness.
It is the voice of hope that will not be stilled

A tiny flicker in a dark place.
It lights the path to a new feeling.

Anger burns and in its flame there is redemption
giving voice to the pain carried for so long.

Silence is broken, the secret told.
It is not my shame. I will carry it no longer.

Forgiveness fills the empty space.
Love of self blooms in the ashes.

And so I begin to create the life I want.
With eyes wide open

Risk the Dark

by M. E. Hart

Sometimes to see the light
   You have to risk the dark
   You have to walk down the alley
         Where the angry dog barks
         Stumble through the forest
            To the sound of meadowlarks
              Slide down the cave
              Where worms and bats gawk
        Dive into the dream
      That has no end and no start
      Forget everything that you
   Think makes you smart
   Look death in the eye
And still make your mark
Sometimes to see the light
   You have to risk the dark

Face down your demons
   In their homeland
   Squeeze out their lives
       With your bare hands
       Stumble through your past
         Where there's no place to stand
        Dive into the depths of a hell
          That would frighten any man
           Walk along the beach

And look under every grain of sand
Crawl along the floor
Like an ant or Spiderman
Fight every dust bunny
Like a high-powered fan
Trying to find your truths
Wherever you can
Sometimes to see the light
You have to risk the dark

Fear not the times when
Living was stark
Look in every corner
Where you see dark—dark—dark
When visions in the night
Froze your body made it lock
Split open your soul
Bleeding and in shock
Wired your mind
For twisted brain locks
Since the days as a child
When soul energy locked
You see, sometimes to see the light
You have to risk the dark
And you have to go alone
It's written in your soul's chart
There are things in life
That for some are too dark
They can't go with you because
They see their face in every tree bark
They are afraid they
Live under every grain of sand

Where you search like an

Ant or Spiderman

Most can't even look you in the eye

And won't shake your hand

They fear the pain and courage

That made you a real man

You see, a man who can't cry

Is a boy in disguise

Who puts on muscles

Trying to hide

Because soul blocks

As a boy made him want to die

When a boy grows to be a man

This truth he must hide

It won't go away

It just festers inside

Society won't help

So the man-boy must fight

He must find his own truths

And just know he's all right

Face to face with his darkness

He becomes the light

You see, sometimes to see the light

You have to risk the dark

Strip off the bark

Silence the meadowlark

Live and make your mark

Even if your start was this stark

Sometimes to be the light

You have to risk the dark...

by Rebecca

I was sitting in Susan's office feeling like the scum at the bottom of a barrel. I had called her that morning and said that I needed help. I had "crashed" the night before and was now as low as I could go. Is this what it took for me to accept that I was depressed? I needed something to help me come out of this haze. I needed to be on medication. I was resistant at first, unsure that I needed it. Now I knew. While I gloomily sat in her tiny office on the plaid couch, we discussed what I could do to stay afloat these next few days. I made a list of people I could call on if I needed to talk to someone—my parents, sisters, a couple of close friends, Susan. I made a list of things I could do that might lift my spirits—get outside, hang out with friends, express my feelings. The only problem was that all I wanted to do was nothing. I didn't want to talk to anyone, see anyone, or do anything. I just wanted to lie there. I couldn't concentrate to do my school work and I had school work to do. I had no appetite. No motivation. Nothing.

A couple of months earlier, in August of 2003, I had arrived in Monterey, California, to begin my graduate studies. I was 26 years old and felt lucky and excited. I was living in a beautiful part of the country, loving the coastline and the weather, the arts and activities. I had finally begun a new chapter in my life, one I had been trying so hard to reach. I was pursuing environmental studies at the graduate level. I had just found a cute studio apartment that had a bed and a recliner and was within walking distance of the school, downtown, and the coast. It was perfect! The only downfall I could find was its proximity to the military base next door. Something about the strength of military men had always made me uneasy and anxious. But I pushed that fear into the back of my mind, far away from myself and my new adventures. I moved in immediately, unloading my full-to-the-brim car, and quickly got settled. I started my classes and met some new friends. I was determined to excel in this program. It was such an intense passion of mine. I was studying to help save the environment! I was enjoying this new step I had taken. I loved everything about it—the town, the school. I even grew to love the sound of taps each night before I went to sleep. Things were good, but like the calm before the storm, a shift happened. Subtly, quietly, things deep within me began to simmer until they reached a roiling boil, and I had no idea what was about to happen.

My nightmares started innocently enough. One night, I awoke suddenly, startled. I looked around and found I was lying in the bed in my studio apartment. The bare white walls stared back at me in the dark of the night. I was lying in a queen-sized bed against the back wall, a bed that constantly squeaked when I moved. Next to the bed sat a dark blue La-Z-Boy recliner. The floor in the main living area was covered with an old gray carpet that was rough like an asphalt driveway. The kitchen was tiny: just big enough to turn around in. It had one of those miniature gas stoves and ovens, perfect for the smallest of spaces. This place was my new home, and I tried to reassure myself before falling back to sleep that I was safe. The doors were locked. I was enrolled in graduate school. I was okay.

But the nightmares wouldn't stop. Suddenly, fast asleep, I would jump up from the bed. Startled and breathing heavily, I had the same dream again, the progression taking me deeper into a place I didn't want to be. In the beginning of the dream, I was moving briskly along a wooded path in the back of a neighborhood. The air was heavy, the night dark, and the atmosphere felt as though it was sitting on my chest. Everywhere I looked trees towered over me. My feet were moving quickly along a path, weaving in and out of trees. I was distraught. Someone was following me. He was a man of average size with dark hair. He was young, maybe in his 20s, dressed in hunter green cargo pants and a black, long-sleeved shirt. He was about 20 yards behind me. I caught a glimpse of a long kitchen knife in his hand. I heard him say my name, Rebecca. He said it almost in a whisper and let it linger in the air. He seemed familiar. Everything seemed familiar, because—as I was about to realize—it was. The next day, I called my friend Marty, who is a licensed clinical social worker. I told her of my reoccurring nightmare. I asked if she thought it had any significance to my past. She told me to find a counselor.

During the summer of 1994, I was visiting home from summer school. I had been spending a few weeks in Georgia at a boarding school in hopes of improving my grades and my motivation in school. It had been a bad year that year. I had had my heart broken by my first boyfriend, had witnessed a tragic accident with my horse, and had learned my mom had breast cancer. I was 16 years old.

On that weekend visit home from summer school, my good friend, Jill, set me up on a date. He was a friend of Jill's boyfriend, and her boyfriend always seemed like a nice guy so I thought his friend must be, too. The four of us were hanging out at Jill's boyfriend's house in the kitchen. I remember thinking how it seemed like the kitchen was made entirely of wood: wooden cabinets, wooden countertops, a wooden table. We were sitting at the table drinking beer. I left the table and my beer, to go to the bathroom. When I returned I finished my beer.

Suddenly, I was lying on a bed in a dark room with a man on top of me. I had no idea how I got there. He was telling me to calm down, that everything would be okay; he was trying to force entry into my virgin territory. All the while I was saying, No, no, no, no, no. Those were my cries for help. No, no, no. That is all I could say or do. I was immobile. I physically could not move. I was literally helpless. My memory came and went; I went in and out of consciousness. There was blood.

When I regained consciousness, my mind was heavily fogged. I escaped. I was unsure what I was escaping from, as my memory was vague. But something told me to leave and to do it quietly and quickly, avoiding all attention. I do not remember anything else about that weekend, the following week, or even the following month. My mom says I wept when I had to return to Georgia the following day. I don't remember. A month later I missed my period.

When my friend Marty advised me to seek help, I did. I came up with a list of professionals and started dialing. I had been to several therapists and counselors before and I knew for this to work I needed to do a screening. It needed to feel right. So I called each person and spoke to each one, or at least tried. Some did not return my call or would only speak to me with an appointment. Some seemed harsh or a little rude. Others just did not seem quite right.

And then there was Susan. I remember calling her and hearing her soft-spoken voice. I remember the feeling that she gave me over the phone, like she truly cared. I knew then that I should at least give her a shot. I made an appointment to meet with her. When the time came to go, I was nervous but curious. It had been nearly 10 years since I was raped. And I had been living my life just fine during that time. But what were these nightmares? What was happening to me?

When I arrived at Susan's office, the first thing I had to do was to fill out some paperwork and take a written test. I knew exactly what the questions were evaluating: What was my mental state? I was feeling pretty good. So when I entered Susan's office for the first time and she proceeded to tell me that I was depressed, it infuriated me. I was not depressed. I had experienced depression and this was not it. She tried to calm my reaction by telling me, "It was just what the test said. Okay, maybe you aren't depressed." Susan knew nothing of my story or recent nightmares at this time. She really did not know why I was there. But I am sure she saw a young girl who desperately needed help and she was trying to keep me from walking out of her office for the first and last time.

I decided to help Susan out, to tell her why I was there. I told her of my reoccurring nightmare. And I told her the very short version of my story. I wanted to know if she thought they had anything to do with one another. And if they did, why was my past suddenly coming back to haunt me? This all had happened years ago, I thought. Hadn't I dealt with this? I had been to counselors. I had stood before a judge, asking for permission to have an abortion. I'd been to a clinic that was later bombed. I'd finished high school. I had gone to college. I spent a summer in Austria. I made friends—good friends. I had had boyfriends, and I had graduated from college, moved to DC, and now was a graduate student in environmental policy in Monterey, California. I was where I wanted to be in life. I was trying to live in the present, live my life, really, and yet I seemed unable to escape my past. But that's it about pasts; they're always a part of you.

That's when I learned about PTSD. While sitting in Susan's office, I learned that day that I had a lot more to deal with than I had expected. Post-traumatic stress disorder, depression, my entire traumatic experience, my inability to feel—the list goes on and on.

When I left Susan's office and returned home to what was becoming the only familiar place I knew, I went online and looked up the books Susan had asked me to order. On Amazon.com I found *The Rape Recovery Handbook: Step-by-Step Help for Survivors of Sexual Assault* and *I Can't Get Over It: A Handbook for Trauma Survivors*. I ordered the two books. I felt really strange. It had been nearly a decade since my traumatic experience. I knew it had forever changed who I was. But I did not understand why, when I had already dealt with it, it was resurfacing.

Two weeks after I started taking my medication, I felt like a new person. Suddenly, I felt alive. I *was* alive. I had feelings. The difference in me was like night and day; like life and death. I couldn't believe that what I was experiencing was normal for most people. And it saddened me to think about how I had lived without feeling for 10 years. I had lived a lost life. But fortunately, that life led me to Monterey and to Susan. Now that I was alive again I had a lot of work to do. It turns out I hadn't dealt with my past after all. I had only survived it and then tried to forget about it. So here I was, sitting across from Susan on her plaid couch in her tiny office, awaiting what was to come. There was a feeling of excitement in me because I knew that things were different now. I was different now. I was beginning a new life. A beautiful beginning.

diligent suns

by S. Kelley Harrell

the wounds rise
like diligent suns
centers of solar systems
I had not discovered
a quick turn around a corner
and my planet becomes sand
on the shore of a dying Universe
it seems the same as apples
a bad one can spoil the whole bunch
yet no one ever knows
which harbors the worm
all they see is the
black hole of its path

Moving Day

by Catherine and her 12-year-old daughter

On January 20, 1997, my young daughter was inducted as a member of a club she didn't ask to join, knew nothing about; she was initiated into this club that does not discriminate, is ageless. A club that the instant you cross its threshold, you remain a member for a lifetime.

You cry at night when you think no one is listening. You cry with the water running behind a closed door where you can wash your face and pat the red from your eyes. You cry hard, and you cry alone.

—CATHERINE'S 12-YEAR-OLD DAUGHTER

I need not tell you about this club, we members know it well, too well, at times. Each is initiated through one's own experience, one's own circumstance; a moment in time is forever ingrained in our minds, never forgotten. Unwilling inductees, we become and remain eternal members of this same club, regardless of how we entered.

With initiation comes an understanding and knowledge only members can truly understand, an experience that also strengthens and empowers. Although membership was forced upon us, we've begun to realize that as members, no one can force us to follow club rules, to conform; we realize that we have the power and ability to decide *how* we want to belong, assigning us a challenge to change the rules, to break them.

Slowly, we're moving in, taking over, rebelling and revolting, changing the drapes, steaming off the wallpaper, painting the walls, remodeling this uninvited club of ours. We're installing a new sound system, modifying the music, creating a new club song; choosing not to wallow and be silenced; we're singing, loudly.

We're changing club rules, compelling us forward, forward as we search for justice and healing; we're insisting on new regulations, reforms, new rules, rules that will prevent/not allow another to join our club.

We were forced to join, so we're moving in...

Our Stories

by Mitzi Soto Albertson

How can you hold in all the stories
Stories of darkness, sadness, isolation and cruelty.
What must you do with these stories?
Do you have a strong chest in which to store them?
Do you swallow them quickly, let them digest and pass?

How can you hold in all the stories?
Stories and tales, heart-breaking, gut-wrenching, soul-twisting stories.
How do you maintain your sanity? Your view of the world?
Do you put them aside and let them decay,
Until their strength can no longer possess you?

How can you hold in all the stories?
Stories of terror, domination, and pain unrelenting.
Do you air them out to dry?
Letting their putrid smell dissipate and dissolve,
So you can view them as what they truly are?
The remnants of the past,
Brought into the light of now,
Never to haunt the future.

How can we hold in all our stories?
They burn us, tighten our chests and burden our souls.
We cannot hold in our stories.
We give them to you, wrapped tightly in a torn, dirty blanket.
A gift for you to unwrap, air out, make sense of...

We give you our stories,
We give you ourselves,
In return, you give us our life.

Vulture

by Dale Coleman

I was about five the first time I met Vulture.
My neighbor had already been raping me in the backyard by then.
I think Vulture knew, enough was enough.
As he swooped down I seemed to know instinctively how to grab on.
I had no fear of him.
It was like I'd always known him.
He didn't swoop down and take all of me.
He just took that inner part of me, the part that could feel the pain.
Perhaps it was my soul.
I remember looking down on myself as we rose, Vulture holding me up.
I could see the pain in my trembling body, but I no longer felt it.
Instead I felt the strength in Vulture's wings as he thrust us higher.
I sensed that he didn't want me to see myself down there as he reached
for the thermal that would take us away.
Once we were high enough we took off in some other direction,
speeding along.
The feeling of flying with Vulture was the most free and
wonderful feeling.
I wanted it to last forever.
But after a while we had to fly back.
Vulture could not keep me forever.
He had come to teach me, not to keep me.
It was then, when he dropped me back in my body, that I knew.
I knew that I could make that part of me fly away whenever I needed to.
After that day I was nearly always able to fly up in the sky when needed.
Years later my neighbor had moved and I no longer needed to fly.

In fact I could no longer make myself fly.
I would lie in the field as still as possible, waiting and hoping that
Vulture would come back for me so we could fly together
once more.
Although he would circle high above, he would not come for me again,
not like that first time.
But Vulture has always been nearby.
He comes to me often but not to fly.
He comes to give me strength.
We will only fly together one more time.
And it will be the last flight for me in this lifetime.

How I Learned to Swim

by Desmonette Hazly, Ph.D.

At the age of 37, the last thing I thought I would be doing was becoming a member of a swim team at a local community college. I had just received my Ph.D., had finished writing a book I had been working on for three years, and was focusing all of my energy on the business I had started and my work as a community advocate. But something was missing. A large hole in my life I had never been able to fill was still gaping.

I am a rape survivor. And as a survivor, I harbored a negative attitude about myself and doubted my own value as a person. I carried heavy emotional baggage that was connected to my body and self-image. The sexual assault occurred when I was a little girl but I kept it a deeply buried secret until adulthood. I went to counseling, but like many survivors, my weight had always remained an issue. Being obese was a choice that I made to hide myself from view and protect myself from ever being hurt again. It did not matter if I wanted to get rid of the excess pounds for health reasons, because I had mentally and emotionally settled on the idea that being overweight was the safest way for me to survive, day to day.

But this was no way to live, and after I graduated from school I found myself wanting more; I wanted a happy, fulfilling life. I no longer just wanted to be a sexual assault survivor; I wanted to be a *thriver*. And I knew that this could not happen if I did not face my attitude toward my own body. I needed to connect heart, mind, body, and spirit to who I wanted to be and move in the direction of healing and reclaiming myself. But I was not exactly sure how I was going to do this. I had no frame of reference for any physical activity, and everything athletic seemed a little too scary to try. I finally decided on dance as being my entry into the physical world because it involved music, and throughout my life, music has always provided me with peace and with a space in which to be consoled. After doing my research, I found myself enrolling in a beginning-level dance class at Los Angeles Trade Tech Community College. My rhythm was way off and I had difficulty picking up the moves, but I realized that I could enjoy physical activity. I dressed in the largest clothes I could find that would completely cover me and I danced in the back of the class so that no one would look at me. I was very fortunate to have found a dance teacher, Diane De Franco Browne, who understood my quest to improve myself and face my fears. On my first day of class, I approached Ms. De Franco and stated that I saw my body as a "necessary inconvenience." As my teacher, Ms. De Franco helped me navigate the mechanics of movement and how it impacts all aspects of life. Over time, I found myself being a little less self-conscious, and I found great pleasure in music and movement and felt comfortable enough to look for other physical activities to explore. And coincidentally, the weight started to rapidly drop off.

I had entertained the idea of swimming and joining the swim team, but I felt I was not mentally ready for such an undertaking. I was sexually assaulted during the summer that I had started taking my first swimming lessons, and I associated swimming with deep, painful memories. I had not worn a swimsuit or swam since I was about eight years old and was not comfortable with having to show my body in public. Although I hesitated and had my reservations, I went to speak to the department chair, Mr. Ratcliff, about classes I could take to prepare me for swimming the following year. Mr. Ratcliff insisted that I had to train with the present team to condition my body and prepare it for the next season. I told him I did not think I was ready and had not swum in almost 30 years. But that did not seem to faze him. I was not about to argue with the chair of the department who also happened to be the head coach of the swim team.

Although my heart sank into my stomach upon hearing this news, I was determined to take the necessary steps to achieve my goal of becoming a competent swimmer and being comfortable with my body. I agreed to show up to the preliminary meeting and be a part of the team. I had to buy my first swimsuit that did not look like a shortened tent. This terrified me, and I ended up buying a suit that was slightly too big because I was afraid of displaying my body, although I had lost over 30 pounds and curves had started to replace flab and bulges.

I had arrived at my first training day in a quiet panic. This was the first time I could not cover up and hide my body. I was surrounded by people who were half my age and far more fit. I felt so embarrassed that I wanted to leave and never return. When it came time for the coach to test my swimming skill, I jumped into the water and felt I was going to drown due to my anxiety. I felt all eyes were on me and there was no place for me to hide. The coach put me in the very last lane for beginners. I felt ashamed because not only was I physically exposed, but also I could not even swim as I wished I could. I was the oldest, the slowest, and always the last in the drills. This was a BIG mistake, or so I thought.

I wanted to quit, and every morning that I went to practice, I silently rehearsed how I would inform the swimming coaches of my departure. But something internal stopped me from giving my notice of final leave of absence. I really wanted to do this for myself. No matter how sore I was or how upset I would be for not being as fast or as competent a swimmer as everyone else, I wanted to see this through. I knew staying on the team would be challenging for me physically, mentally, and emotionally, but it was time for me to move on despite my fear and anxiety.

I tried very hard to understand my relation to physical activity. I found that dancing and swimming are very much alike; timing, space, and distance are essential for success. And one needs to be completely in tune with the body to achieve the desired outcome. I had never been in tune with my body. My body and I had been through a bitter divorce, and I was not expecting any reconciliation, so I had ignored it. Trying to reestablish communication with my body after not speaking to it for so many years proved to be my biggest challenge. I was emotionally paralyzed from the neck down and, in my own way, learning to walk again.

I found it hard to comprehend my body in relation to space and timing, and the basic skills of swimming seemed to elude me quite often. I could not learn the techniques without a major battle with myself and my wounded ego. Every time I thought about my difficulty with swimming, I became angry because I had to fight and struggle so hard for something that comes so naturally to everyone else.

My coaches were unaware of my reasons for pursuing swimming or of all the emotional baggage that accompanied me on my aquatic quest. Sometimes they seemed to be bewildered by the extreme frustration I had toward my own perceived inability to master the skills like everyone else. Cheri Swatek and Tom Bristow were very patient and indulged my intensity. They would repeatedly go over the proper motions and timing exercises. I always felt desperate to have some sign of great improvement, and I subjected Coach Ratcliff to endless questions on how to get better. He always patiently assured me that I was doing just fine. I often told my coaches I was officially the adaptive student of the team because I just could not catch on to things the way I thought I should. But I stayed, nonetheless.

Every day got a little better, and I became just a little faster. Not as fast as the rest but not finishing as far behind the others as when I first started. I was gradually gaining ground, second by second. When it came time for the swim meets, I was always scared out of my mind but found the courage to participate even though I knew I would come in last. I would climb the starting block and feel I was about to meet certain doom each time I dived in. It pained me to always be last after having put in so much time and energy. I did not want to participate in the final swim conferences because I knew how each race would end. But life is full of beautiful surprises. For my 50-yard butterfly, I came in second to last. Not a big deal for anyone else, but a huge triumph for me. And at the end of it all, I finally understood what swimming meant to me.

My swimming coaches, Joseph Ratcliff, Cheri Swatek, and Tom Bristow, were teaching me not just how to swim, but how to live my life without limitation. They gave me a gift I never thought I would ever receive: a life of fitness, confidence, and self-awareness. Swimming has become the metaphor for reclaiming my life, and these are my swimming commandments I have come to live by:

1.   If you take the risk of challenging yourself, you will never fail.
2.   You are worth the time and effort needed to improve yourself.

3.   Always keep moving; stopping means being passed by or run over.

4.   Defeat means only that you have more work to do.

5.   Expect the best from yourself and always deliver.

6.   Tough times are opportunities for greatness.

7.   Always know where you are so you can get to where you need to be.

8.   If you go the distance, you will never have any regrets.

9.   If you let go and just be, the rest will take care of itself.

10.   Victory and triumph are what happen when you know you have given it all you've got.

Beauty that is

by Beth Smith

Looking down at the scattered pieces on the ground
she sees beauty.

A menagerie of shattered glass
the broken pieces of her life spread before her.

Bending over to pick one up the sharp edge cuts her deep,
standing in the middle she weeps.

She places that piece on the board then picks up another
her hand will be raw when she is done.

Arranging the pieces in a window, making them shine
in the sun.

Light cascading through the pain, and anger, the tears, and joy
cleanse the pieces of their hold.

She stands back to see, the beauty that is, from the pain that was.

Anger

by Sabrina Francesca Manganella

I am about ready to throw this saucepan in the trash. Just one look in the pan made me gag, and I had to hold myself up over the sink until my head stopped swirling. I soaked the pan before dinner, but it looks like the blackened bottom is permanently fused to thousands of bloated rice kernels, bunched together in a milky puddle of water. I take a deep breath and grab the SOS and start scrubbing.

When I scrape the fat rice kernels off, they slide around the dishwater, touching my bare hands. My face purses up involuntarily, and I yank my hands out of the water.

The past overtakes me in strange moments.

I can see Jack lying on the couch with the cat on his stomach, scratching her ears. His eyes are smiling as he listens to the receiver. There is a long pause and then I hear him say, "Did you see the game last night?"

I look around the kitchen. Dishes are everywhere. A half-eaten roast chicken leaks bloody fat off the cutting board, and onto the dirty kitchen floor. Turning my back to the sink, I wipe my wet hands on my apron and walk into the living room toward Jack.

"I am not your maid," I whisper-spit at him, my hands on my hips, like an old shrew.

He smiles at me, and holds up his finger to tell me just a minute.

"Go ahead, laugh and tell jokes while I scrub the pan." I stick my middle finger up at him and go back into the kitchen, slamming the door behind me. I feel like taking this pan and smashing the house to pieces with it. I get back to scrubbing the pot.

Then guilt washes over me. Why did I scream at him? We were having such a happy evening. Did I have to stick my middle finger up? What kind of wife does that?

I take Wellbutrin to make me less pissed at the world. My dopamine levels are artificially up, but to say I struggle with anger is a polite way of saying that somewhere out there, probably lying on their couches, surrounded by their loving families, are two men whom I would love to pummel into the ground. Bloody and screaming they would beg me for mercy, but I would not give in until they realized the total impact of their brutality. But no amount of pummeling can teach them the errors of their ways. The worst thing about hypocrites is that they really believe they are the good ones.

They must have seen something in me when I was a girl, my vulnerability, my loneliness, my willingness to please, and they pounced. They took me at different times, breaking my spirit like you break a horse, making me obedient, crushing me, and crushing me again, teaching to me be saddled, bridled, and whipped. I learned to take it. In fact, I learned so many lessons that don't work in a world where a man isn't lingering around every corner ready to tear me to pieces.

After I load the dishwasher, I go out to the back stoop and sit, trying to breathe slowly like I learned in yoga.

The gardenias are starting to bloom. When I planted them seven years ago to hide the air conditioner, they were only about a foot tall. Now they are trees, towering over our heads, and we have to cut them back every year. Soon the branches will turn limp, heavy with virgin flowers, white and bursting with a scent that covers the whole yard with innocence.

I bring our neighbors armloads of flowers and they always say, "So many!" their eyes shining at the excess. After a couple of weeks, the blooms turn brown, but their fragrance remains until all the withered petals fall to the ground and the bushes turn green again.

I can hear my daughters' clear birdsong laughter carry from the side yard, hearty children's laughter that fills the world with goodness. I need to run, need to stop the churning that threatens to boil up and burn my family.

When Soki, our little black dog, sees me putting on my sneakers, he starts wagging his tail and getting underfoot. I tell Jack, still on the phone, that I will be back soon, and he waves.

The girls are making some type of soup out of flower petals, grass, and chalk. They barely look up as I run out of the yard.

Soki pulls me onward, his face open to all that might come next. I wish I could see the world through his eyes, a feast of smells and people to lick. I run past little brick bungalows with wide porches pushed up next to each other. I wave to a dad sitting on his porch, watching his baby daughter play in their sprinkler.

In some neighborhoods in Africa, when a woman gets raped, her neighbors hunt down the man who tried to make her soul disappear. They tie him up, carry him to her, whimpering and begging for mercy. Then she beats him silly, as her friends and family jeer.

In America, there is no cry of outrage after a rape. Instead, there are hoops to jump through, and they are so small, so hard to squeeze through, that your will to fight shrivels, paralyzing you. Of course there is no evidence. There never is.

I run past a peach stucco storefront church, filled with black people singing, their hands raised. Inside there is hand-painted sign that says, "Dare to Thrive in 2005." I want to thrive, like the gardenias planted by the air conditioner. I want my gifts to blossom from my life with fecundity, like fragrant flowers, freely given and exuberant, blessing those whose lives they touch. I want to let go of my anger, let it drop from me, like withered leaves, leaving room for new growth, new healthy buds. Yet how do I let it all go? My anger seems to have embedded itself into my being.

I head into Daffin Park. There is a wide jogging path that surrounds the park, but I like to run through the grassy promenade, lined with live oaks. I sprint through the tunnel of arched branches until I reach my favorite tree. Then I lie down on the cool grass.

While Soki happily sniffs, I look up at the leaves and the dangling Spanish moss. I let the breeze touch my sweaty body. My hair is frizzy and my face is purple, but I don't care. The only thing on my mind is the way the tree branches hug over me, protecting me, comforting me. They whisper to me silently in words only my spirit hears.

When I get up to run home, a little girl, frozen in time, starts screaming. I can see her, carrying an old baby doll in the garden, dreaming of running away to Never-Never Land.

Once she climbed a tall ladder and stood at the top, repeating, "I believe, I believe, I believe," daring herself to jump, daring herself to fly. She stood there for a long time, holding on to the top of the ladder, looking down at the floor below, waiting to find the courage to escape.

Finally she climbed down slowly, ashamed and defeated. Her scream echoes through my body, as she revolts against some long-ago fight that she lost.

She lives inside of me with another girl, a lanky, punk, clove-smoking teenager who writes streams of stories about being fatefully misunderstood. Her sanity is hanging by a string, and that string is a lie. The lie keeps revealing itself as such, but she blinds herself and holds fast. It is the only way she knows to hold her mind intact. She blames herself for every outrage perpetrated against her.

These two clamor for attention. Drowning in confused anguish, they hold their hands out for help. They are still waiting for rescue. I am the only one who understands them, their story. I hold the key to their comfort, but I can't find it anywhere.

Rape victims. Survivors. Whatever. They are noisy, and I wish they would let me get on with my life, which is relatively normal.

I know my life doesn't sound normal—since I've just explained that I have these two children living inside of me. But I really am normal. I mean most people don't know that I have this going on. I could be in the middle of an enormous internal crisis and someone could call me, and next thing you know, I would be talking about Karl Rove and his evil plans like the rest of you.

I walk over to the lake. It is only about four feet deep and has a cement bottom that is covered in green feathery fuzz and rusty cans. Tonight there are at least three families fishing in the setting sun, waiting for some disease-infested fish to grab onto their bait. They glow in the peach light.

I head over to a bench and sit down. Soki smells every bush he can, chases a squirrel, and then walks back and stares at me, his eyes asking, "What now?" I don't have an answer for him. I don't know what to do now.

I'll be vacuuming or doing the dishes and my mind will turn to these men, and I will fixate on one of them, and I will start writing the perfect letter in my mind, the letter that will turn this ghost into a shriveled-up human being, stunning him into understanding. Then I get stuck on what I would say. What can words do now? They don't penetrate. I want to invade him with my maggoty words, which will feed on his soul until his brain is filled with hungry flies. But no, my words are the air that holds my story and nothing more. If he was dumb to my screams of terror, blind to my shocked eyes, then what could my words do now?

My anger swims inside of me, a shark in an empty fish tank with no one to eat. I can go from woman of the year to a screaming lunatic in less time than it takes to realize that dinner needs to be made and there is no food in the house. My daughters are little kids, and act like little kids, and therefore become a wonderful repository for my anger. I blame our justice system for my bad temper tantrums. I think my kids will just blame me when they get old enough to see me for who I really am.

When I feel overwhelmed by some miserable task at hand, I go into a mode that can be best described as Total Bitch Mode. My daughters will be innocently playing some elaborate pretend game that involves taking all the pillows off the couch and chairs, all the blankets off the beds, and making some island in the middle of the living room floor. This island is often covered with almost every one of their toys that has lots of little pieces.

So they are full on into some complex pretend scenario game and then there comes their mom, who has been ignoring them all morning, and she is in Total Bitch Mode. How do they feel when I ask them why they have to make things so difficult for me? How do they feel when I ask them why they have to make such an enormous mess and then expect me to pick it up? They feel bad. They were having fun. Now, out of the blue, their mother who is supposed to kiss all their tears away is furious because they made such a mess. They must be bad children, they think.

I see myself and hear myself and I know I am behaving immorally. I am harming their little souls. Fury bubbles up in me after years of swallowing it down with the other liquids I was forced to swallow. Yet I am not the child anymore, and I am not in danger anymore. My children are.

One time, after going off about some ridiculously innocuous thing the kids did, I apologized to them, and said Mommy was going to really try to not get mad at them for little things anymore. My four-year-old looked at me and said in an unflinching tone, "Don't try, Mom. Just do it."

Medusa and her tangles of snakes for hair—you know she got those snakes after Neptune raped her. Her glorious beauty was encapsulated by her fury. Am I turning my daughters into stone, when they have to confront my anger? Are they becoming harder, emotionally, building up a barrier to protect themselves from the pain my anger inflicts on them? I want those snakes to go away and I want my hair back. I want to be beautiful again.

I watch the sun fall over the dirty lake.

When I get home, the house is dark except for the light of the TV. Jack lies on the couch, an opened Corona on the coffee table, watching football.

"Are the kids in bed?"

"They want you to check on them."

Savannah is already asleep. Mary is awake. I kiss her on her forehead and she grabs hold of my hand.

"Stay with me. I'm scared without you here."

I sit on the bed and she wraps her soft brown arms around my sweaty hand. How do I know when to ease her fears and when to leave because I am just teaching her never to go to sleep without me? How can I be the mom I so desperately wanted when I was a little girl? My mom always said she tried as hard as she could. Empirical evidence shows that her parenting based on "trying hard" was completely ineffective. What more am I doing? I'm trying as hard as I can, just like my mother.

After a while, Mary's eyes shut, but when I try to pull away from her, to go sit with Jack, she grabs my hand tighter, letting me know she is still awake and still needs me.

Whose hand can I hold onto for safety? Whose neck can I wring? What path can I follow? Was the mother and wife I was born to be ripped away from me, never to be given back? They took away my childhood, but can I give them my family to gobble up, too?

There is no path in sight, only my meanderings to Daffin Park, the endless one foot in front of the other, holding out hope that one day my soul will open up wide enough for the rage to spill out, leaving space for my own rich laughter to spring forth.

fighting cholitas*

by Liz Cascone

slam this poetry
say it, sing it, shout it
your ears will hear it
and you will doubt it
shall i stand in front of this mic
to hear my voice crack
stage fright
in my sneakers
i'll clear my throat
speak truth untold
feedback from the speakers
feel my lips tingle against the cold
metal makes vibration
my voice will shake this fear
but my words jumbled and unclear
we're gonna get personal tonight
so let me introduce myself
hold tight
i am no pussy
drive a nail through my heart
i will keep walking
and stalking you
to find my voice
as i go hoarse
a story with might
i speak through stage fright

my long tail keeps the balance
a hard hat covers my chalice
like a shell, live to tell
and raise a boy
to see humanity
born a blank slate
before the jedi mind fake
confuses a man's sanity
makes them rape all femininity
can he be a man that interrupts
the cards dealt for heartache
that's what's at stake
i curl into a ball
from winter to fall
but summer i open
stretch, stand tall
i crawl onto this stage
to share this rage
let's have a ball
this is a mind-bending
gender fuck
i'm a girl with relatively little luck
this is a story
told without any particular glory
born a common girl
without realizing the common story
that makes us warriors
armored fighters
it's the chipping away of spirit
that happens each night
let's give some examples
prove i'm right

age four
my protector
even with, he touched my lips
a relative stranger
all i remember is your
fat belly against my hips
age seven
you hid in that white coat
beneath your stethoscope
this is what you get
spread your legs to disinfect
mom said, step into your armor girl
you'll need it, that's for sure
lay your head against the pillow
close your eyes to see your guide
age thirteen
i had a dream
called seven minutes in heaven
locked the door with my neighbor boy
wound up labeled a whore
age sixteen
you sling jokes at me
bra snap provokes adolescent glee
it's a trap, the joke's on me
call me sensitive
when i don't agree
don't think it's funny
try being a girl
i'll pay you money
cause you couldn't last
in this cast of refugees
age eighteen

tell me your name
cause without it
i got no one to blame
and that night you seduced me with reggae, right
no woman no cry
such an ironic fight
i walked five miles that night
down five forks road
not yet set in, my shame
just want one touch to be right
gentle and slow
yes or no
i'll let you know
your pace at my pace
head back
let go
age thirty-three
woke up from a dream last night
your hands between my thighs
they scream
my body shocked from being naïve
your face still rough
a shadow of midnight
hickey stained skin
marked as possession
i've had enough
so, that's how a girl's story goes
each is different
but everyone knows
no woman no cry
as irony dies
see, we can't be

authentic and free
we're sold as a commodity
bought and bargained
disguised by pop culture jargon
beat up and fucked
our bodies stuffed
with plastic and fluff
i purge my disgust
i will never trust
fight i must
the curtain falls at dusk

The Fighting Cholitas are a group of female lucha libre wrestlers who perform in El Alto, Bolivia.

Bitter for the Sweet Child Within

by Nazneen Tonse

Tiny bud of a child, do not uncurl
Fight your soft petals' yearning to unfurl
Young flowers risk grooming by thoughtless hands
Picked and pruned, some sent chilled to other lands.

Tiny bud of a child, why must you bloom?
Petals are always crushed to make perfume
You'll be but a smear in their folds of flesh
In their thirst for the innocent and fresh.

You are just the bloom that precedes plump fruit
They will pluck and suck and strip to the root
Amused, they use you and leave you to cry
Crawl to the dark and wither yourself dry.

Tiny scab of a child, gather your seed
In wait of a time when you may be freed
When she screams at memories and flings them far
Fall to earth, take hold, and show her her scar.

Choose earth that is hard, unwanted, concrete
Stepped over by a world of busy feet
Be a weed of the sort gardeners despise
Survive the cracks and catch a poet's eyes.

Up from the Ashes

by Kathy

Most spiritual journeys start out with a bang. After eight years of therapy, I was still feeling restless and frustrated, and I needed a deeper level of healing. My very core still felt wounded.

A therapist suggested I try a technique that eliminated the spoken word and bypassed the intellect. The therapist highly recommended something called *rebirthing*. A good friend, who had experienced group rebirthing, provided the phone number to a healing center. Within a week, I participated in my first rebirthing session. Rebirthing became a pivotal fork in the road of my healing journey.

I was initially scared and uneasy about rebirthing, but hopeful. The sessions consisted of one hour of talking and one hour of deep conscious breathing with a coach. Deep conscious breathing, using something called cleansing breaths, requires breathing in through the nose, then out through the mouth. From the moment I took the first breath, I received clear, disturbing memories. My body shook, and I knew immediately that this experience was going to be different.

With rebirthing, the memories of my abuse were crystal clear, as if I was watching a movie in my mind. Up until this point, I had only had flashes or small glimpses of a scene. Rebirthing put me on notice that I could no longer deny or hide in the shadows. I had always had doubts about my memories, somehow thinking maybe I had made everything up. Now I began to realize without any doubt that my father had sexually abused me. I remember being beaten, choked, and raped like an animal. His behavior was very confusing because by day he pretended to be a loving father; at night he was a rapist. I followed his patterns of pretending. I had never remembered what was real until now, many years later.

On many occasions during those abuse incidents, I felt close to death. My father rode me like a grown woman. He forced his penis into many parts of my body. He would put his hand over my mouth so I would not scream. In order to survive, I consciously left my body and focused on the ceiling. While he abused me, I remained in my mind and pretended to be someone else in a different place. I know now that this approach kept me alive.

At times, my father seemed to look right through me. He would call my name or sometimes call me baby. I hated when he called me baby. I would think internally that I was his baby daughter not his baby. He just wanted me to be there for him, no matter what. He took what he wanted from me. Because of the abuse, I felt invisible and felt I did not matter. In my mind being seen meant pain. There was plenty of pain, tears, and blood. Through the rebirthing sessions, I started to remember all the details. I became suicidal and death seemed easier than to acknowledge those memories.

To cope with my feelings, I began binge eating. Overeating was an old friend and I was out of control, again. I ate huge amounts of food to cover up feelings of shame and guilt. I had to focus my attention on overeating and feeling uncomfortable in my body to allow me to continue to live. I felt ashamed and dirty. My rebirthing coach told me about spiritual bathing. After the sessions, I would take long baths with sea salt and baking soda. Sometimes I would take two baths a day because the water was very soothing. I looked forward to taking baths and it became a daily ritual.

My feelings escalated and I began to disassociate, lose time, and isolate. Friends would beg me to socialize, but I wanted to stay away from people. I stayed at home, primarily in bed. I got up only when necessary, such as when I attended regular therapy and rebirthing sessions, and when I needed to take care of financial matters. After that I went back to bed. I stayed in bed so much I wondered if I had experienced a nervous breakdown or if I was healing.

I recalled several memories of oral sex with my father and this bothered me greatly. I became so nervous and out of control I starting excessively brushing my teeth and washing my hands. This pattern became very prevalent. Eventually, I could not leave the house. I felt crazy. I thought people could see the semen on me. I felt like a dumping ground and a cesspool. I did not want to be seen.

I increased the rebirthing sessions and traditional therapy, but no matter what I did, I woke up with thoughts of killing myself. These feelings were so intense that I thought I would be in therapy forever.

I often wondered if I would ever get better. How could I contribute to the world or myself? I was at my lowest point of despair. My rebirthing coach told me something that would change everything. She said I could never physically wash off the memories. The abuse had happened a long time ago, but I could never wash off the residue. I had been trying to wash away what had happened. I felt dirty in the deepest part of my soul. My father's semen was in every part of my body and no amount of bathing, teeth brushing, or hand washing would ever change that. Instead, I needed to heal my broken heart. I cried throughout the entire two-hour sessions. I cried so much that the tears stained my face. But as strange as it may sound, I think the crying helped cleanse my soul and spirit. My emotions came from a very deep level. I knew about the sexual abuse, so why was I still crying so much? The rebirthing coach explained that I was healing at a deep level, and I was actually getting better.

I recalled my hands being tied and being alone in the basement, and I finally understood the full level of cruelty that had occurred. The memories were devastating and pushed me closer to suicide. The rebirthing coach kept reminding me that the events happened long ago and that I had already survived. These memories had come up, she said, so that they could be healed.

I continued the baths and began to recite positive affirmations. I practiced forgiveness exercises by writing affirmations of forgiveness 70 times a day for seven days. I began to put a new focus on my journey. I spoke only to individuals with positive or supportive attitudes. I learned to recognize and honor this healing process. Once a week, I would show up for the sessions and work my way through deep-seated memories. Somehow, through the pain, tears, and suicidal thoughts, I managed to look into the eyes of the rebirthing coach and know that she cared about me and my healing. I began to trust her, and I hung on to whatever she said. If she told me to repeat affirmations and write them one hundred times, I followed her instructions to the letter. She was my only hope. She told me if I worked through the painful memories, I could climb out of this abyss. On many days, I felt worthless and not deserving of the air I breathed. My self-esteem was at its lowest point. It took a tremendous amount of courage and faith to get up and move away from the darkness.

My thirst and my deep desire to heal helped to propel me forward, until one day I woke up and realized I had gone from darkness to light. There would be no more emotional roller coaster or lying in bed. Now my heart was filled with peace, love, and serenity. I kept reminding myself that I was okay. I had survived the healing, as well.

Somehow, I thought maybe what I had been through might help others. I started to tell my story. At first, I began with small groups, women's shelters, and hospitals. The editor from a national newspaper heard of my experience, requested an interview, and published my story. After the story ran, I received calls from abuse survivors from around the country. They applauded me for having the courage to speak out. The journey was long and at times not very pretty, but it was well worth the personal growth I eventually gained and the peace with which I now live.

by Jackie

I loved the air, the sky, the grass, the trees. I loved smelling all the life that sent droplets and mist and juicy, pungent, or sweet aromas all for me while I played on the swings or in the sandbox or among the trees with friends to hide from or tag. When I laughed I would take in big gulps of energizing breath, giving me even more joy to play in. I know I felt good in my body. I was eager for life and joy. My energy flowed from me, connecting me with the sunlight, the stars, the clouds, the flowers, and the earth under me, whether covered in snow or pine needles. I was in a state of complete un-self-consciousness. I was as whole as a girl could be.

When based overseas, my family traveled a great deal. My mother wanted to show us the world, and that she did. She would take me and my sisters camping for whole summers—no brother or father, just us girls. I loved being in France where the young women would dote on us and paint our toenails on the beach. In Spain a mountain caught on fire and we all had to go down to the water with our rafts to stay safe. My mother made it a game and we felt excited, adventurous. We were all so taken with the world. In Germany we would hike or drive somewhere new almost every weekend. The air was crisp and wet on the mountains and when I took it in, I felt it made my insides green and mossy.

No one had to teach me to breathe then. Breath flowed through me like summer breezes through an open window, graceful and spontaneous, even with parents who believed "spare the rod and spoil the child." Mostly my parents would forgo the philosophical and would hit, pinch, and pull hair out of pure anger and, ironically, fear of losing control. I know this put fear in me. That was the point. So, my playful days were often punctuated with spasms of fury. But still, despite the confusion and hurt, I was a spring sapling with golden energy running through me, brimming over.

What force then, what blow it took to pull the breath out of me. He pulled it out by the roots and kept pulling until my lungs hung hollow and shriveled in my vacant chest. He was the thief with our father's smile, stealing life itself. I remember leaving my body—this same body that climbed me up trees, that rolled me down grassy hills, that swam effortlessly in lakes and oceans. I gasped, I choked, and just before leaving, I froze, suspending me for years between nightmare and nothingness.

I wonder, when you were a boy, who took your breath from you? When you came back from Vietnam, what unmentionable traumas captured your life force so that you chose to take mine and my sisters' from us, as if it would replace what you were missing?

For me, shame is the lived sense of insignificance—of being rendered into nothingness, made so unimportant that I do not even have the right to breath. I have heard that if we stop breathing, we die. But I swear, there were days, months, maybe even years when I didn't breathe. Breathing would mean I meant something. It would mean I was visible and present and neither of those options was viable if I was to survive.

I do remember one bright, peaceful morning. It was summer vacation, and we had traveled overnight to visit my aunt and uncle in Maryland. After hours of darkness, I opened my eyes to see the sun rising, scattering gold beads across the suburban lawns of my aunt's neighborhood. Everything looked so peaceful and predictable. I felt as though I was in heaven where everyone was safe and kind. I knew that while we were there, my sisters and I would be free from my dad's touching. I did dare to breath that morning and with the breath came the beauty of the day.

It is many years later, now, and I am rediscovering my breath, my being. It came first like breathing in fish scales, rough, jagged, and foreign. I wanted to scream with each conscious inhalation as my throat constricted to say, "STOP! STOP! It's not safe!" I resisted it in my yoga practice—always skipping over the inward practice of breathing. Over time I began to allow myself to peak at the breath, nibble it, sniff it, and follow it quietly in and out. I started to experience the compassion that is the seat of breath, and I knew that was the way I was to return home to myself.

Breath is the ribbon that holds me to the baby self, the girl, the teenager, the young mom, the therapist I am now. The silky blue ribbon of breath threads through my past into my present and through all the breaths I have yet to take, making me present and whole. Breath flows through me again like the river that smooths the jagged rocks, making this once-glacial lake a fertile valley. I am brought to myself, the self that has always been here—alongside the shame, terror, grief, and aloneness, I have been here. I am here now.

With presence are memories that appear like curious surprises on the landscape. It's similar to driving in a neighborhood with which I am well acquainted when, all of a sudden, I see a beautiful house that I have never noticed before. I am seeing and understanding my experiences and loving myself as I go. I am seeing myself as brave for trying to stop my father from touching my sister. I am cradling myself as I remember what I did to survive the anguish of a torn body. As an act of love, I am giving myself the gift of breath.

Now, as a therapist for traumatized children and families, I am reintroducing boys and girls, mothers and grandmothers, fathers and stepfathers to their breath. Some children I see are like gazelles in the tall grass—they are frozen, breathless, and alert. Others are in constant motion, as if centrifugal force will clear the way for them to find safety. I invite them to return to their breath. I safely reacquaint them with the place where breath lives inside them, still, always. We do mountain pose and warrior pose and the balancing tree and we breathe to be present and whole. We, together, feel our roots growing back.

Sometimes Angels

by M. E. Hart

Sometimes angels
        have got to remember to fly
Especially after we think
        parts of ourselves have died
Our wings get heavy
        and fold in at an awkward bend
Our thoughts get
        caught in an internal whirlwind

Weeks stretch to years lost in work before we know
    And we forget to fly, forget to let go

Dust in the corners
        and things left undone
Remind us every day
        of the moment we started to run

We run, walk away from everyone
        or maybe we half-heartedly try
But we never face it down
        Step up to the cliff and fly

Sometimes angels have got to remember to fly

If we don't

> we stop
> we stay
> we die

Remember to fly

> Please, a plea, a whisper, a sign

> > Please, remember to fly...

The Forest of Life

by Sara

As we walk through the forests of our lives, there are many paths we can choose. Some paths take us in circles, leaving us to roam aimlessly and never bringing us to the cozy, warm campfire that we want—a haven of safety. There are the paths that lead to high, dangerous cliffs, and if we aren't careful, we may fall. Occasionally, we encounter people who cross our paths. We greet each other momentarily and continue along our own chosen paths. On other paths, we meet fellow hikers who walk beside us for a while. They camp with us and build fires in our souls.

Sometimes the path is blocked with fallen debris from others, such as my dad's alcoholism, my mom's violence, and the sexual predators, all of whom still haunt my mind. These elements left scars that are deep and still visible. Occasionally, the scars are reopened and they ooze a nasty pus that stops me in my tracks so that I have to cauterize them before I can move on. Debris like that veers me off onto paths along high rocky cliffs that are dangerous, and I am scared, hungry, cold, alone, and lost. One wrong step and I could plummet to my death.

Sometimes in the forest, I have broken tree limbs and turned over rocks, only to find poisonous snakes and scary insects. I have come upon bears and wolves who thought I was food. Parts of the forest are haunted. Ghosts follow me and whisper ghastly messages in my ear. To make myself brave in the face of such danger, I used to drink alcohol. Everything would become confused. Alcohol really made matters worse. I couldn't seem to get a fire started. Eventually, I would stumble into a camp with people like me who drunkenly had found their way to the same safe spot—a special camp. We would look at the map of our lives again, and find out how we had followed the wrong path. Together we would blaze new trails.

On the new trails, we would come upon an occasional forest fire, but working together, we were able to extinguish them. Together we learned that by taking just 12 steps from where we stood, we could find better places—places we never knew existed. We found ourselves on paths we never believed we would walk.

We walked together for a long time on the same path. As we each got stronger, we made different choices in the directions and paths we would follow. Yet no matter where we went, we carried the others in our hearts. They continued to give us strength.

Paths inevitably lead to clearings that provide a place to rest and rejuvenate. Here, we have time to think about where we are and where we want to go. We make plans and set goals. This can mean saying good-bye to those we have traveled with for many miles. In the future, we may cross paths again. These meetings bring news of others that meant so much to us at one time. Receiving news brings happiness as well as sorrow.

It was one of these times that I learned of Dana. Dana was a warrior. She braved a lot and came out successful. Unfortunately, she never felt the success. Her paths were never easy and Dana began to choose the most dangerous paths. She was caught in a twister that spiraled her downward and cast her off onto the cold, gray rocks. She got lost under dark and gloomy skies. The ghosts that whispered evil words in her ears grew loud and forceful. They became the only voices she could hear. She died. She died alone. They didn't find her for three days. She was all alone. I don't think she knew that people cared about her or that she was loved and missed. This news distressed me, and I thought, "But for the grace of God, there go I." I imagined Dana lying on her bed, dead. When I look at her face, I can see a shadow of my own. It scares me. Why didn't she send a smoke signal? Given the same situation, would I have fired a flare? Would anyone have responded? Would the haunting ghosts have prevented the signal from reaching out?

I've been on that path. I have learned to reach out. However, there is always the chance that when the path gets extremely tough, the rains become tempests, and the ghosts circle about, I will surrender and throw myself into the ravine, where I will lie dead upon the rocks, and no one will find me for three days. I hope I can stay off that path. If I can't seem to avoid it, I hope someone cares about me enough to throw me a rope and pull me out.

News isn't always sad. There is good news when couples join, when children are born, where mountains are scaled. This type of news brings hope—hope that I can reach that mountaintop, hope that I can make it through the forest and find a nice cabin in the woods with loving people, a warm fire, and a cool stream nearby.

Knees

by Paula Hodgkins

When I was little
my knees were always together
until he forced them apart
against my will

When I had my first menstruation
I was so thin
my knees knocked together
like skeletons

When I was in college
my knees were always apart
it was the only love
I knew

Now there is so much fat
on my knees
that they are always together
my protection
from unlawful entry

Shrapnel

by Deb Sherrer

sex u al(l)
abuse or violence
like a **B O M** *b*
that ex-
plodes
leaving shrapnel
embedded in your psyche
memory frag ments
dissociated at first
in the blast
then working their way
to the surface
in nightmares
trigger-hair flashbacks
leaving you like a vet
shaking, catapulted into terror
when a car backfires unexpectedly
a smell, touch transporting you to the edge
of control
the ripples in your nervous
system
begging for release
waking you at 4:00 a.m.
to write

Grooming

by Mary Zelinka

I wanted to hate Pop Randall, but by then I loved him too much.

And I needed his world of horse smells every bit as much as I craved my mother's thin split pea soup when I was sick. Horse manure, hay, fresh sawdust. The sudden dry dustiness of the grain bin as I climbed inside, searching out soybeans to suck on later. Pop's cotton shirts smelling relentlessly of Pall-Malls, no matter how many times his son Henry washed them at the laundromat.

The pervasive scent of a horse during a workout. Sweat foaming from under the saddle and the reins where they rubbed against an arched neck. Sometimes when I rode, that thick sweat soaked into my socks. When I got home I'd carefully wrap them in waxed paper, savoring the sweet-bitterness until my mother discovered them under my pillow and tossed them into the wash as though they were dirty.

Horse shows brought their own smells. Neatsfoot-oiled saddles and bridles. The sharp metallic of polished stirrups and bits. Ginger.

I had ached for horse smells even before I knew they existed. At four, I scoffed at the other children shooting one another with Roy Rogers cap pistols. The empty holsters slapped stupidly against their thighs and dirty strings strained at their necks against bouncing cowboy hats. I galloped alone. I'd throw my head back, toss my hair, and whinny.

My sister Gracie thought my games were babyish, but once she played horses with me all afternoon. Then a real horse pranced down the street ridden by a girl who couldn't have been any older than Gracie. Gracie watched until they disappeared, but I ran behind the house crying because my horses were only pretend.

The slap of the screen door and Mother calling, "Girls, it's Howdy Doody time!" echoed in the dusk's stillness, but I stayed out on my swing, scuffing my Keds in the red Carolina clay. I leaned way back, until I could feel my hair stirring the dirt. My insides cold and empty, I stretched my hand toward the pale moon. *If only,* my heart pleaded. *If only I was the girl on that prancing horse.* I arched my back, clenched my hands into fists around the ropes, and swung hard, kicking my feet at the moon.

We moved to Florida before I started second grade. Paved sidewalks separated Miami's lawns and there were no woods to hide in. So I pranced around our block with a Tinkertoy bit between my clenched teeth while the other children made fun of me.

When I was eight, Father took the family to a horse show. I don't know why— we never went anywhere together. We sat in the stands watching riders parade their shining horses in front of a man wearing a suit. The man smiled at the riders and rewarded them with silver cups and long ribbons.

Then some horses, picking their feet up high in the air, trotted into the ring. "Five-gaited American saddlebreds," Mother read from the program. I stared. Long graceful necks curved their heads close to their chests. Eyes wide, nostrils flaring, ears twitched forward and back. Long legs brought knees high and then hooves neatly tucked before briefly touching the ground again. Tails swished like flowing scarves.

"W-what's that s-smell?" I asked Mother. A sharp odor had suddenly cut right through the earthy horse smells.

"Shush!" Father glowered at me. Mother patted my leg.

Years later I would learn that heady odor was ginger. Grooms chewed the white root before inserting it in the horse's anus so he'd carry his tail high during a horse show. I would learn, too, that the excitement of horse shows came at an even higher price than the burning sensation of ginger. Trainers cut the saddlebred's tail between two vertebrae and when not being ridden the horse was confined to a harnesslike tail set. After Henry told me the horse eventually lost his ability to switch flies, I begged Pop Randall not to cut any more tails.

But at that moment, watching those high-stepping sleek horses, I didn't know about tail cutting. Or what it would cost me to become one of those straight-backed riders.

I stuttered so badly that normally I never risked asking for anything. "I can't understand a word she says!" Father always shouted. But after that horse show, galloping around my block wasn't good enough anymore. I begged until Mother finally allowed riding lessons.

Horse smells then became my life. Key Lime Stables, home. Ma and Pop Randall and their son Henry, four years older than me, family.

At first, Mother waited in the car while I had my lesson, like the other mothers. "Up-down-up-down-up-down," Ma Randall hollered as she ran alongside the thick-necked pony while I posted clumsily. Later Mother dropped me off early in the morning, driving back the 7 miles after I had exhausted myself from a day full of riding and grooming horses. By the time I was 10, I ran beside the beginners myself, calling, "Up-down-up-down-up-down," in my best Ma Randall voice. I didn't have to beg Mother to buy my lessons anymore. Instead, I earned them by helping the beginners and cleaning stalls.

Key Lime Stables was primarily a training barn. Pop bought green American saddlebreds and then turned them out as polished three- or five-gaited show horses, reselling them after one or two successful shows. We had a team of riders ranging in age from 12 to 17, but I got the most attention, probably because I worked so hard.

"That girl's got more energy than sense," Ma said. But she smiled when she said it. When there weren't beginners to teach or horses to cool down after rides, I tagged after Pop. I'd hold the twitch so the horse wouldn't move while Pop clipped his ears, or I would stand next to Pop as he coached Henry or one of the other show riders.

Henry and I sometimes unloaded hay together, sliding bales as fast as we could across the smooth haymow floor. And as Henry hauled manure out of stalls, I replaced it with wheelbarrows of crisp shavings. Sometimes I'd perch on the tailboards that were mounted inside each stall to keep the horses from rubbing their tails against the walls and watch Henry, tall and lanky, spear his pitchfork into the old bedding.

Most of the time Henry ignored me as though I were a pesky younger sister, but sometimes he'd toss a "road apple" at me. This would start a battle quickly escalating into a manure-throwing frenzy, stopping only with Pop's hollering, or with Henry slinging me over his shoulder and dumping me into the water trough in the back field.

Penny, or Penelope's Desire, was my favorite. Nearly 17 hands high, she was a blood bay, with a thick black mane and tail. She'd just turned three, and Pop hadn't started riding her yet. I stood close to Pop as he exercised her on the lunge line. "Look at that," he said, as she circled us on the long rein, picking her feet up high. "All that is natural action. Just wait until we put weighted shoes on her and see what she does. She's gonna make a dandy five-gaited horse—hard to beat."

"But then you'd have to cut her tail," I said.

"Pah! Nothing wrong with that. That's just part of grooming for a show horse."

"She could be a pleasure horse," I countered. "They don't have to have cut tails." Penny trotted steadily, but she eyed us as she circled and twitched her ears as though she were listening.

"She's too good to waste on that," Pop said, and the subject was closed for that day.

"Do you think I'll ever be good enough to ride her?"

"Sure, someday. Here," he handed me the lunge line. "Keep her steady." He clicked out of the side of his mouth at her. Pop stepped behind me, keeping his hand on my shoulder so that I would stay in the same spot as I circled with Penny. "Keep grooming her. She'll get to trust you."

Every day I groomed Penny. I'd pick up each hoof, carefully cleaning it with the hoof pick, pressing my fingers over the fleshy frog to check for signs of thrush. Then, making small, quick circles over her coat with the hard rubber curry comb, I'd bring all the dirt to the surface. The stiff brush whisked it away. Her deep red coat gleamed like copper after a quick rub with an old feed sack. I hand-picked her tail, one hair at a time, so it would stay thick. Once done, I'd lead her around the stable and let her eat grass.

When it rained I'd lie on my stomach on the tailboards in Penny's stall and she'd twitch her lip across my back, sending shivers down my spine. The rain chimed down on the metal roof.

Weekends and holidays I was the first one at the stable, sometimes surprising a sleepy-eyed Pop, his coffee in one hand, the hose in the other as he refilled water buckets emptied during the night. I'd race up to him, knocking him off balance as I flung my arms around him. "Well, good morning, Princess," he'd always say, his cigarette pinched between his lips. I'd take the hose to finish watering and watch him amble off to the feed room to mix grain, his boots polished under his tan jodhpurs, suspenders over his white long-sleeved shirt with the cuffs rolled up to his elbows.

Pop or Henry began picking me up after school and taking me home after I rode. I often went with them to supper at Howard Johnson's. Sometimes I stayed overnight.

The Randall family stories became as familiar to me as my own. I knew that when Ma Randall was just my age, she had climbed the wall at Al Capone's Miami Beach home so she could watch his parties with all the beautiful ladies in their satin dresses. Pop had fallen in love with Ma at the Miami Charity Horse Show after she won the Championship Amateur Three-Gaited. She ran off and married him when she was only 17, even though he was older than her father.

I knew Pop trained horses in his sleep because I could hear him dreaming in the next room when I stayed over. Henry sounded like a big cat purring; once he had fallen asleep against my shoulder as Pop sped us down the freeway in his big yellow Buick after a horse-buying trip.

Just after my twelfth birthday I rode in my first horse show. I still have the black-and-white 8 x 10 glossy of me on Dark Destiny taken by the show photographer. I'm wearing a tan riding habit an older girl had outgrown. My left wrist drops a little, a bad habit I had not yet broken. But it's the look on my face, the intense ecstasy, that now brings tears to my eyes.

Moments after that picture was taken I was awarded a long, red, second-place ribbon. Ma beamed at me from the other side of the ring, and Pop met me at the gate. Henry took Destiny's reins as I slid from the saddle into Pop's arms. "Good ride!" he kept saying, hugging me tight.

A few days after that first horse show, late in the afternoon, I followed along as Pop pushed a wheelbarrow full of grain. I'd lick my finger and dip it into the mixed grain, sucking the sweet bran that coated it. Pop scooped up a bucket and told me which horse to take it to. I'd hurry it into the stall so he wouldn't get too far ahead of me. When we were done, Pop leaned the wheelbarrow against the wall inside the feed room. I folded the empty feed sacks, relishing the feel of the bristly burlap.

Suddenly, Pop stepped close behind me, pulling me back into his chest. He fumbled quickly at my belt. Then his cold, thin, callused fingers slid up my shirt and squeezed my brand-new breasts. Breathing hot in my ear, he whispered, "Are you my little Princess?"

Scrunching my neck against the chills, I pulled away from him. I could hear Henry pushing a bale in the loft overhead, beginning to hay. I looked into Pop's watery blue eyes. He was smiling.

Henry drove me home that night. "Hey kid," he said, tugging my ponytail, "how come you're quiet for once?" I shrugged my shoulders and leaned against the car door, my eyes blurring the passing lights.

The fluorescents seemed unusually bright as I walked into the kitchen. Mother stood at the sink peeling potatoes, a yellow apron tied in a bow around her flowered shirtwaist dress. I looked down at my dirty brown jodhpurs, beginning to fray over my scuffed boots, and felt my face go hot with shame.

"Go take your bath, Mary Helen," Mother said without turning around. "Dinner's almost ready."

Without getting undressed, I filled the tub and sat cross-legged on the floor next to it. Leaning on the edge I watched my fingers make circles in the water. Then as the tub drained, I took off my clothes and put on clean pajamas.

I never again called the Randalls Ma and Pop. It seemed like Mrs. Randall didn't smile at me so much after the feed room day. I worried that Mr. Randall had told her about my breasts. I stopped following Mr. Randall around, but he always seemed to know just where I'd be anyway. That moment in the feed room blurred into countless others.

Years of horse shows and the pungent smell of ginger followed that first long, red ribbon. Silver cups and trophies with golden horses perched on top filled my bedroom. Younger kids vied to groom my horses now, and to walk them after I was done with a workout. I rode Penny in her first horse show and in time we became regular winners in the Saddlebred Pleasure class, where the horses did not need to have cut tails.

When I turned 14 my tan show habit was replaced with one tailor-made. Navy blue, it had a bright red satin lining that flared out as I rode. Mrs. Randall accompanied my mother and me to a store, across from racetrack, to be fitted.

A jockey was there at the same time getting new silks. The tailor's thumb pressed one end of the tape into my crotch as he measured the inside seam while Mother and Mrs. Randall chatted. By then I was accustomed to having a man's fingers in my crotch and a lot more. I looked across the fitting area at the jockey who had the other tailor's thumb in his crotch. His eyes bored right through me. Then he grinned.

Almost 30 years passed before I spoke of the feed room moment and its aftermath. I was at a training on child abuse for my work at the Center Against Rape and Domestic Violence. After we paired up, the facilitator instructed, "To help us remember what a child's world is like, close your eyes and think of the happiest time of your own childhood. Then the saddest. After a couple of minutes, I'll ring this bell so you can share with your partner."

> I was twelve. The late afternoon air danced golden in the dimness of the feed room. I could hear the horses munching grain as Henry dropped leaves of hay into their hayracks. My tongue tasted like sweet bran and the empty feed sacks felt wonderfully rough as I folded them. Pop smelled like cigarettes and hay.
>
> But his breath was hot in my ear when he whispered, "Are you my little Princess?" My nipple turned hard when he squeezed it. I wanted to hate Pop, but I loved him too much. So I mumbled, "Uh huh," and hated myself instead.

I looked into the eyes of my assigned partner, a woman I had just met. "It wasn't your fault," she said.

Over the years I had said those exact same words to countless survivors. But until that moment I had not understood that they applied to me, too.

I'm Telling

by Donna

How often in a day does one sibling say to another in a sing-songy sort of way, "I'm tellll...innnng!" Ten times? A hundred? Plenty. Those two words hopefully strike enough fear in a brother or sister to stop whatever they're doing, or else. The "else" could mean parental intervention or retribution. Many start early—the search for justice.

My father told me, after every rape, "You tell anyone, and I'll kill you." For a long time it worked. And then it didn't.

The progression of my telling began with a tearful, whispered confession to a close and trusted friend 20 years after the abuse ended. Within a decade it had morphed into a telling that was like a dark woolen cloak I wore everywhere. I found myself telling almost anyone, anywhere, short of clients and store clerks, something to the tune of, "Hi, my name is Donna, and I'm an incest survivor."

Eventually my voyage from the maze of silence to the wide-open freedom of voice brought me to a place where I was able to transform my experience into a work of art. I took my muddy, stinky, slimy mountain of pain and confusion and turned it into a bold, sparkling offering about my evolution and clarity.

I've written a one-woman play about surviving incest and my journey toward wholeness. Not only did I write it—I'm performing it every chance I get. I'm telling like crazy. And boy, oh boy, does it feel good.

My first performance of the play took place a few years ago at a residential school for sexually reactive and abusive boys and youth. Seventy boys, ages 11 to 20, were in the audience, sitting on the floor in circles of eight with each group's clinician sitting with them. The faculty and administrators lined the sides of the gymnasium.

Are you getting the picture? Me, an incest survivor, standing at a microphone, telling my story to a gym full of boys who have committed the crimes of my father—one way or another.

I can't describe, in this short essay, everything it took to get my body straight and supple enough to speak into that microphone. But I can give you a taste.

Once I decided to "tell," by writing a play, words began flowing out of my pen like a mountain creek at the break of spring—fast and fresh. Some mornings I'd wake up an hour earlier than usual—no alarm clock, just my itchy fingers stirring me.

There were lots of roadblocks along the way. Here's a journal entry after two months of writing:

> Here I stand, an empty vessel inside a sealed glass tube, scared shitless that the best of what I have to say got said in the first twenty pages and it's basically downhill from here. I will just keep descending into deeper and deeper silence. Whatever fire was burning in my belly to heat up my words is out or, at best, nothing but cooling embers.
>
> The Pollyanna in me wants to say, "Blow, girl, blow on those embers. Ball up a sheet of newspaper and throw it in. Rebuild the fire."
>
> "Aaa, ha," says my inner critic, "there you go trying to pretend yourself into believing you can resurrect what's gone. Nice try."
>
> And then a glimmer of an idea breaks through—like a tiny beam of light leaking through a chink in the brick wall of a dark basement. This internal dialogue has something to do with Dad telling me he'd kill me if I told. I've been telling bits and pieces—on paper, in my journal, in my writers group—for a very long time. But now I'm fixing to tell a whole bunch more to absolutely anyone who wants to listen.
>
> Do my father's words, his threats, remain alive in me? Staying ready to pounce the minute I look the other way? Pounce on my fire with steel-toed work boots, kicking the logs apart, peeing on the flame?

If this is what's happening to me, if this is why I haven't been able to get back into writing, then I'm really angry. I know it's really, really important to not be angry at myself because that will only prolong the anger. And the anger will prolong finishing the play.

Here's another journal entry, about a year later:

I make myself sick every time I walk toward what I know I have to do. Sick with fear. Fear that I'm about to ruin my life by writing the play. Life as I've known it. A life I've become accustomed to, safe in, confident with, sure of.

Through this long creative process it has helped tremendously that almost everyone I tell says what I'm doing is brave, smart, and needed. But all the well wishes in the world can't eliminate the fears. As they emerged I wrote them out in my journal. Here are a couple that reared their heads in year three:

Fear #1. Once I get it all written and blocked and rehearsed, then one of two things is going to happen. Either no one will show up or plenty will and none of them will be moved. They'll leave the performance, heads slanted into each other talking about how they hope I didn't quit my day job.

Fear #2. Sometimes, when the playwriting's going really well, my whole pelvis feels like a strong set of white wings keeping my spirit high and mighty. But there's also a scream tucked in the cup of my pelvis on the right side.

There are moments, muddy water moments, when I hear a distant echo of that scream burrowed down under my right side. It makes my ribs quiver. Mostly the rib quivering happens when I sleep. Some

mornings I'll wake up, roll over onto my right side, and get a little jolt that feels like a thumb pressing into the middle of my rib-
cage, always on the right side. But, at that moment, my thumbs are
nowhere near my ribs. Usually, by the time my feet hit the floor, this
question of where the hell that annoying pain came from is pretty
much out of my mind. Except for a couple drops of consciousness
that know it's "the scream."

I believe the scream is one long endless wail for all the abuse that's still
happening. Even with all the memoirs and TV specials and Bishops
Commissions, every minute of every day, in every place where people
live, it's happening. No matter how many times I get up in front of an
audience, open up the veins to my heart and tell my story through the
play, the "everywhere abuse" is still going to be going on.

The problem is, if I pay more attention to the scream than to the
play, I'll probably stop working on the play. Which means that I cut
off my contribution of a thimbleful of water dropped into the well
a bunch of us are trying to keep filled in the middle of this parched
desert of neglect.

A little internal demon of emotion presented itself along the way on this path to
"telling." Some call it the inner child. Mine's an eight-year-old girl—I named her
Molly many years ago while getting counseling for the incest. I was slightly familiar
with her, but we hadn't had many deep conversations. To be honest, I was pretty
afraid to hear just how mad she was with me for some yet-to-be-named betrayals
and transgressions.

I had a hunch this was a key to unlocking more that I wanted to put in the play.
I needed to coax Molly out: out of my body and my mind into the light of day. I
suspected that whatever she was holding onto was keeping me from telling everything. Once again my journaling led the way.

I've just spent three pages writing what I'm going to write about instead of writing it. Just goes to show you how remarkably hard this particular interior conversation is going to be for me.

What I ought to do is just try to imagine Molly's here in the room. She's behind the black couch crouching under the piano bench. She's sucking her thumb half in a trance and half listening to every word I'm writing. Nothing, really, gets past her.

As long as I'm sitting here judging her, she's not going to move one muscle, not say a word to me. This is so frustrating. Geez—it's like I'm having a group encounter all by myself on this page. My inner critic is having a heyday, telling me I'm doing this all wrong.

Ooooooooo, she just moved from under the piano bench to the chair with the yellow and blue floral print. Her hands are holding onto the arms of the chair. Her legs are doing little kicks, bending at the knee. She looks at the toes of her shoes as they rise before her. Serious. Her little face is so serious and a bit expectant. She doesn't want to let on that she wants to talk.

I try to keep my breathing regular and calm. I let my hands rest gently on my lap, no sudden movements. I take a deep breath and tell my voice to stay soft.

"Hi, Molly."
She glances quickly at me and then returns her eyes to her peek-a-boo feet, saying,
"Hi."

I tell her,
"I'm glad you're here. I really want to talk to you."

"No you don't."

I say to myself, "Don't get defensive, don't overpower her, connect with her."... I take a deep breath.

"Are you mad at me?"

"Yes."

She twists a handful of the hem of her dress—a blue and green cotton plaid with a white collar turned gray from 50 years of neglect. Our eyes touch for half a second before she looks down at her busy hands.

"You went to help Mom."

"Is that why you're mad at me—for helping Mom when she had the operation?"

"How could you? She didn't help us."

The critic lands a karate chop on my notebook, yelling, "An eight-year-old would not say a line like, How could you?

See? See what I have to contend with? See why it's taking so damn long to write this damn play? See?

This would be the beginning of a series of internal conversations between my grown-up self and my wounded child, all helping to traverse the way to the peace of self-acceptance.

Long before I got a director for the play, even longer before I found a master guitarist to accompany me, his music calming the atmosphere down or stirring it up as needed, I read my play to Liz. This member of the Sisterhood of the Traveling Survivors was also a writing companion and one to be trusted with my trembling offering.

She perched herself on my couch—eyes wide open and sharp as laser beams. I stood 6 feet away from her, my play in one hand, pen in the other.

On the second page I got an idea and started writing in the margin. Liz jumped off the couch and said, "Gimme that," reached up, took the pen out of my hand, sat back down on the couch, and said, "Keep going."

Every time I got choked up and lost my place, stamped my foot, or growled when I flubbed a line, she'd say, "Just keep going."

The whole time she sat super erect and never took her eyes off me, even when they filled with tears. When I was all done, she jumped up and down, gave me a big hug, and said, "I'm so proud of you."

Then we ate lots of chocolate.

I did 15 more readings—to more writing companions from my writers' group and selected friends, two or three people at a time. Each time I took more pauses, lost my place less, moved more loosely in my body, felt less frustration when I got choked up, waited a few more beats if there was laughter or tears, breathed deeper as I turned each page.

To begin and guide this journey of creation I wrote out my vision for the play:

> I see the play describing some of the pivotal moments that got me going. I want to tell the audience about the things that took a long time and a lot of work to get me through all my pieces of the healing. I want to be funny and make people laugh. I want to be poignant and make people cry. I want to be inspiring and make people brave. Brave enough to speak—even if the only one they are speaking to is themselves.

> I want them to consider the possibility that everyone can do something to break the silence and end the cycle of violence. I want to pick the right stories of my journey and string them together in just the right way so the audience will be uplifted by this subject instead of disturbed, or worse, more numb than when they came in the door.

> I want to tell my story of surviving incest. I want the context to be more about my resurrection than his crimes. Tell all I've done to be my fullest self, not just what he did to hurt me: to focus not so much on his destruction as on my triumph.

I've performed my play eight times over the last fifteen months. Every time I perform it I heal a little bit more. The silence is breaking apart and my creation is weaving my self back together.

by Nick

My day in court was memorable.

He looked quite insignificant when I saw him. I knew it was him instantly—he still wore the same parting in his hair. The belt with the large, shiny buckle was as unmissable today as it was back then.

But the dynamic had changed. The power dynamic. I saw him through the lens of a man, a 6' 3" professional businessman. He looked small and insignificant; the clothes he had changed into when he was moved from prison to the court looked grubby. I remember the parka jacket from way back. Why was he still wearing it 15 years later?

His barristers were outlining their defense. One of them was a boy I had gone to school with. I wondered whether he, too, was one of the "chosen." I felt repulsed that he was defending such a man.

There had been others, many others, in the intervening 15 years. Only a few of the braver ones, like me, had agreed to run the gauntlet of the trial. My brother, a fellow victim, decided that the prospect of it was too much.

I felt quite pleased to be there. Freddie, the policeman assigned to my case, and I got on from the moment we first met. His clipped professionalism slowly ebbed as we learned to trust each other. Freddie had given me enough clues that I began to understand that my offender was a career pedophile, that the man's insatiable appetite for children—all boys—had led him to rape his own innocent kids.

I felt sorry for my offender as I looked across the dock. He looked dejected. How could anyone think that having sex with their own children was okay?

He faced questions from the defense barristers. He didn't understand why boy "X" would suggest that he'd abused him orally. The picture that the police had found in his wallet was not because of his obsession with the lad, he protested, but because he had found the picture on the playground of the school he was caretaker of; he'd planned to return it.

The details of the cases spanned decades, but the stories were excruciatingly similar. School, Cub Scouts, camping, canoeing, baths, gifts, sex. I felt anger. I felt angry at myself for being taken in by such as he. I remember looking up to him when I was 11; he was my missing father, my strong protector, my pathway through the horrors of adolescence and my abusive mother. He was taller than me, stronger than me, hairier than me, cooler than me, and he loved me. I kissed him after one of our sessions because I loved him back.

I felt anger at my inadequate parents, anger at myself, anger at his wife for sitting downstairs while he exploited our innocence in the upstairs bathroom.

She was in the witness stand, telling everyone how wonderful he was. The perfect husband, the provider, the daddy to their three children. She must have known. My day was Thursday. My brother's was Wednesday. He had boys for every weekday. Every weekday, we'd disappear for hours upstairs. While she watched the soaps, I was getting lathered up: washed and scrubbed with particular attention being paid to the undercarriage.

I felt hate. Self-loathing for being the co-producer, the willing accomplice, the explorer. I felt hate for my insatiable desire to find out more and for my ability to keep our secret. I couldn't feel hate for him that day in court. I was unable to, not yet; those emotions would only come many years later.

Because it's better to keep dangerous emotions in, stiff upper lip and all that, don't want to create a scene, do we? I felt hate for the parents, mine included, of the Cub Scouts group, parents who failed to make a scene back in the 1970s but instead decided it would be for the best if he stepped down as leader of the local troop, no questions asked.

I wanted to shout obscenities at his wife while she gave evidence. You KNEW! You f**king KNEW you lying b**ch. I felt sorry for her too—30 years of marriage and all she has to show for it is a pedophile husband and three broken children. I felt guilt that my actions had brought that on her.

Recess. Cigarette. Coffee. Fresh air. The boy from my school, the defense barrister, and I met in the corridor. I tried to avoid his eyes but he acknowledged me as we crossed paths. I felt sickened that he knew how naughty I had been and how dirty and unlovable I was.

A chat with Freddie: he thinks things are going well. Not much of a defense, eh?

I look back on my day in court and a decade later now realize that while externally I might have looked like a professional businessman, I spent the day as a frightened 11-year-old. I remember little more but recall the foreman of the jury reading out the guilty pleas. Sentencing was delayed for reports. I couldn't make it to the committal proceeding. I couldn't face him again and only heard the next day that he'd been sent down for five years. My emotional dam broke four years ago; I let the anger out through counseling, a baseball bat and a punching bag. I feel nothing for him now; the bond between us is broken.

I am a man; a successful, gregarious, intelligent, humorous, powerful, individual, caring, loving man.

I am free of you.

I love my life.

I love myself.

Thank You, George

by Larry Conrad

This is another one of those occasions where I find that I am writing too late. I knew you were ill with cancer, George, but frankly, I did not yet have what I wanted to say framed clearly in my mind. I was also still lumbered with many of the negative images I had of you from when I was a teenager. Though you and Lois were among Mom and Dad's best friends and you personally always treated me well, I felt uncomfortable around you.

There was a big reason for that, and I will get to that in a minute. But I was also a struggling teenager with confidence issues, and your very tall stature, your shuffling gait, your free and easy manner, and your sharp and sometimes really gross sense of humor made me feel ill at ease. I didn't know how to behave when you were around. I never knew what to expect from you or what you would say next. And when you paid attention to me, I would usually become so confused I just wished for some trap door to open under me so I could fall through it and escape.

But you were a good and decent man, and I just hate admitting that I didn't see that. Or maybe I just didn't pay attention to it—I don't know. But you bestowed a precious gift on me one summer, a gift that took me decades to understand and appreciate. This is why I am writing to you now.

Do you remember that in the spring of 1964 you bought that terrible dump of a house in Steelton? This was another of your "projects," and I remember you being so excited about it as you described it to Dad. The house was a plum for the picking, you thought. It needed so much work that no one would buy it; the price was therefore very low, so you snapped it up with the idea that you would make the necessary repairs, rent it for a time, and then sell it and make a tidy profit. Wrong!

The more money you sank into that house, the more it seemed to demand; it was like a financial black hole. By the time you had finished the external work you were overextended and didn't have enough cash to hire anyone to deal with the interior.

That's where I entered the picture. My mom handed me the phone one evening, and it was you: could we meet the next day to "talk business"? I immediately felt uncomfortable, but clearly you wanted to offer me a job of some kind. I know you meant well, George, and I also recall you telling me that you had already run this past my dad and he had said it would be okay. Almost any other boy would have been delighted at what you were about to propose to me.

But George, I wasn't just any boy. I had been sexually abused from the age of 10 until I was 14, and when you called me I was 15. That was only a year after the abuse had ended, and I was an emotional wreck. I trusted no one. I was afraid and anxious all the time, and I felt absolutely worthless, or rather good for only one thing. I simply could not imagine that I had any skills, merits, or talents (except for "that"), and as you talked to me the next day, I was overwhelmed by what you said to me. You offered me a summer job repairing and painting the interior of that house. You named a fixed price for the job, and you assured me that while I would be working on my own, you would always be just a phone call away, and if I ran into problems, you would explain things and help me.

What an opportunity for a 15-year-old boy! I was too young to apply for working papers, but now all of a sudden I had a good-paying job where I would be on my own and could set my own schedule and—this was important!—play my transistor radio as loud as I wanted all day long. How totally, totally cool!

But I reacted with fear and disgust, George. I thought, "Look at this, even my dad's friend can figure me out." It never occurred to me that you were really going to trust me with such a job, relying on my abilities and assuming that I would be responsible. Instead, I thought the fee you named was what you were willing to pay for me to make myself sexually available to you all summer; the house would just be a place where you could help yourself whenever you wanted. But by then I had no boundaries and zero self-esteem, so after my initial negative reaction I got practical and thought to myself, "Okay, it's not like I don't know how to do this. At least this time I will get paid."

So I accepted.

As the first day of the job approached, I sank deeper and deeper into self-loathing and despair. I wished I had killed myself years earlier, as I had planned and attempted when I was 11 and then again when I was 12. I lay in my bed at night filled with horror, thinking, "It's going to start again now. I can't stop it. It's not up to me." I felt like I was being dragged into some terrible machine that would mangle and destroy me, yet leave me intact for the whole process to be repeated the next day. The hell of abuse was closing around me again and I could do nothing to escape.

That first day, my heart was racing as I got on my bike. I had a change of under-wear with me, of course; I just assumed you would hurt me as bad as you could. That's what sex was, after all, or that's what it was as far as I could see; it was what adults do when they want to hurt a kid. I was flooded with feelings. Maybe you would kill me right on the first day; how merciful that would be! I hated you for figuring me out, and I hated myself for being me. My self-loathing swelled as I rode down to Steelton. You want sex with a teenage boy? Okay, I will show you things you never dreamed of.

So imagine my surprise when I walked into the house to find you shuffling around amid piles and piles of paint cans, brushes, rollers, drop clothes, tool kits, sandpaper in many grades, wood, nails, saws, hammers, etc. Before I could pick my jaw up off the floor you had your arm around me and were walking me through the house talking about color schemes, offering ideas for repairing and replacing bad woodwork, and complaining about faulty old plaster here and there. At first I thought, yeah right—we're just heading to the bedroom. But no. We blitzed through those rooms like we did through all the others, and soon we were back down in the kitchen. You opened the fridge: I had never seen so much Coca-Cola in all my life! You told me to help myself and to let you know when the fridge needed to be restocked. Then you tossed away the lunch Mom had packed for me and showed me a scrap of paper on the kitchen table. Written on it was the phone number for a little Italian place down the street. I was going to get hungry working so hard, and you insisted I should eat well. Whenever I was ready for my lunch, I should just call the restaurant or go down and see what I wanted; they would run a tab for me and you would cover it. No baloney and cheese sandwiches on one of George's jobs!

You asked if I had any questions. My head was still reeling and I didn't know what to say. Then you just wished me well, reminded me that I should call if there was any problem at all, and went out to your truck and drove away. You just left! You hadn't touched me in any inappropriate way; you hadn't mentally undressed me; you hadn't cornered me or groped me...nothing! I don't know how long I stood there alone in the living room, totally confused and trying to think what I should do next.

I did finally figure out that you really did expect me to paint and fix up this house, so I started and soon I got into a daily routine. I would work away as rock music blasted from my radio, practicing my dancing as I painted (my friends Barb and Franny had taught me how to dance that spring), sipping Coke all day long, and exploring the delights of Italian cooking. I really got into the job and soon I was loving it.

But there was one thing I could not understand. What were you waiting for? I was there for the taking—any time. Each and every occasion you showed up to check on me or to answer my questions, I thought, "Okay, today he will make his move." And when you didn't, that confused me. What was wrong? Did I look scared? Was I ugly? Did you think I would tell? Why would I do that? No matter how many times you proved how safe you were, I kept telling myself that you were just playing it cool. Things would start one day soon.

It went like that all summer. I finished room after room and the house really began to look nice. I felt appreciated and I liked it when you were pleased with my work. I tried to concentrate on my job and wished you didn't "know" about me. But...you must know. Otherwise, why did you ask me to do this job? Sometimes I would look around at my work and want to feel proud, but I couldn't. So many days I stopped and cried, wishing I wasn't a whore and trying to figure out what was wrong with me. Again, as when I was younger, I wanted to crawl away into a corner or find a place to hide.

At the end of the summer I was finished early and had the whole house clean and ready for the flooring to be done. I wanted you to see I had done good work; I wanted you to like me. And I didn't want you to mess with me. "Please don't fuck me"—the phrase rang in my head and seemed to echo through the empty house.

There was only one more day. "Please. I don't want this." But it seemed too much to expect. My heart was racing again as you looked over the house and raved about my work and how clean everything was. You offered to take me home, and I thought, "Aha! Here it comes. He will do me in his own house. Now I get it." But instead you threw my bike into the back of your truck, we piled in, and you drove me home. In my driveway you paused, pulled out your wallet, and gave me a generous tip. I don't remember the amount, but it was a lot for 1964. Then you shuffled back over to your truck and drove away.

You were gone. The job was done. Nothing had happened. What was going on? I didn't get it. I was confused and I ached inside. I liked the idea that I had done such a good job, but I hated being me. What was wrong with me? Upstairs I collapsed onto my bed in tears. Was I so ugly? Why didn't you want me like Mr. ____ had? I felt abandoned and lost. I was overwhelmed by my feelings, and fear just crashed over me. What was happening to me? I remembered praying when I had been little and I thought of doing it again. But I was too scared; "God only lets this happen to retards and rejects." Mr. ____ had told me so himself, and he must know; he was a big deal in the church, or so I thought.

It's been 46 years since that summer. I regret to say I sank a lot lower after that, George. Alcohol and drugs almost finished me, but that's not why I am writing to you. I have been clean 35 years, as of this past Fourth of July. I married in 1981 and have a wonderful family. Both my kids have gone to college and are doing well, and I entered a career as a university academic in a field I love. I was not able to begin dealing with my abuse issues until late in life, but I am doing well now. I know what happened to me wasn't my fault, not in any way. I have jettisoned most of my bad feelings about myself and every year I am more and more at peace with who I am. I am happy, George. It's okay to be me.

But where is all this going? As I began working in therapy and seeing how utterly false all my old childhood feelings about myself had been, I began to look back and reflect on that summer. I began to think about how—no matter how well you treated me—I still expected the worst. That realization showed me the terrible, tight grip that the false lessons of abuse can gain over a boy. I began to understand that these lessons don't just go away when the boy grows up and becomes a man. I could sense the difficulty of the task before me. But at the same time I was learning that I had been worthwhile, special, and important all along. I had not seen it, but you were a good man. You cared. But you cared because I deserved it. I was an innocent defenseless boy, not the tough guy I thought I was, and you looked after me because that's what good men are supposed to do. This revelation was one of the many I wept over in that stormy first year in therapy.

In the course of my professional work I have also had the opportunity to work with many young people, and most recently with young men struggling to deal with the terrible burden of sexual abuse. So many of them feel as I once did: that the abuse is their own fault and that they are worthless and good for only one thing. But every time that subject comes up, I tell them the story of painting your house in the summer of 1964. I use it to show the guys how all the bad feelings they have about themselves can feel so real and yet be so completely false.

And you know what, George? They get it. They really do. They love the image of you shuffling around and telling me which color goes where, while I stand there astonished, expecting something else entirely. It sticks; they remember it. When they once again fall into the trap of believing those old false feelings, all I have to say is, "Well, remember what I told you about...," and usually I get interrupted with a laugh and the comment, "Oh yeah! George's house!"

I recently read a discussion on the question of whether things happen for a reason. Do they? I'm not sure. But George, the kindness and generosity with which you treated me that summer have turned into something far larger than either of us. It has become a symbol that I can use to convey a message of hope and healing to others. It's a beacon that shines across the years and allows others to see that the fight is one worth fighting and that it can be won, regardless of how destroyed a survivor thinks his life is at the moment.

I regret I was not far enough along to tell you all this yourself before you died. I didn't yet understand. But that utterly broken boy of so many years ago sees more clearly now. Both he and I want to thank you. I will always remember your gift, which was perhaps all the more colossal because you bestowed it upon me, and now upon so many others, just by living your life to its fullest potential—as a good man.

Sunshine and Rainbows

by Lorraine

He was my uncle by marriage. I thought I trusted him. I was nine years old. It tore me apart. I had nightmares. I was scared all the time. I pulled away from people. One of my teachers took me aside to find out why I had changed. He knew something was wrong because I stopped talking. It was hard, but I told him what had happened. He tried to help me by encouraging me to express myself. He said, "If you can't find someone to talk to, just write down your feelings." That is when I started writing poetry. My teacher was the only one I told. I found out my uncle raped his own daughter after he raped me. She told on him and he went to jail. I thought it was just me, but then when I found out I wasn't the only one, it made me feel a little better, especially since he went to jail. I just want people to know that you aren't the only one out there this happens to. You can get help to get through it. Tell someone you trust. It really helps.

Some people abuse you because you have a disability. They may think you can't do anything so they take advantage of you. I have a disability, so I know. Some people look at the outside and not the inside. Who you are on the inside is more important. People with disabilities have a heart, just like everyone else. People can't just abuse us and get away with it.

I had two friends at the community workshop where I go. A cab driver had started touching me in a sexual way. I went to tell my friends and found out that he had been touching them also. We found a safe person to tell who helped us report it to the police. We all testified in court and he was sentenced to four years in prison. It was really hard to do this. My friends helped me through this difficult time. I didn't want him to hurt anybody else, so I had to do it.

It is important to have someone to go to if you need help with your problems. With help, I have found the sunlight inside of myself. I have gotten past the bad feelings and feel the sunshine and see the rainbows. The person who believes you and helps you is important. I found someone to trust and she helped me a lot. She helped me more than she will ever know. Look and see the person who is helping you; see the sunshine in that person. Because of this person, you are not alone. I hope that when you read this you will know that people with disabilities are sexually abused, we can go to court, and we can get help.

Nature's Healers

by Pamela Brendel

Who are these people
This rare breed
Who can open their hearts
To all the pain and suffering
in the world

Who are these people
That become our positive parents
That show unconditional love
Who won't leave us
Blame or shame us

Who are these people
Who show us our strength
Our courage, our power
When we can't see it on our own
Who see the goodness in us
When all we see is bad

Who are these people
Who pull us up from total despair
To heights we never dreamed of
Who've shown us all the reasons to live
When we just wanted to drown

Who are these people
That treat us with respect and dignity
When we feel we don't deserve it
And show us our worthiness
When self-doubt is all we feel

These people are one of nature's greatest gifts

They are mighty oaks to show us strength
Weeping willows to allow us to feel
Bleeding hearts to share our pain
Thorns to prick us into reality
Roses to spread the beauty of life
Ponds to give us tranquility
Compost to nurture and seed us with hope
The sun to warm our empty hearts
And most of all they are us, at a different place
And we know, one day
We'll be there, too.

Thanks, to all the therapists who counsel survivors.

There Is Hope in Healing

by R.

Let me begin by apologizing for two reasons. The first apology is because, much like other narratives written on the broad topic of abuse, the content of which I write is not pleasant. The second apology is because I have allowed my strong and capable voice to be silenced for so long. I deeply apologize (mainly to myself) for not having spoken sooner. For decades, it has been my alliance with writing and art that has helped me survive, but until recently, my words and artistic endeavors have remained relatively private. Through a promising albeit intense therapy process that utilizes art in healing, my stories are being transferred to spoken words and meaningful artwork. It is a process that is liberating me from remaining ensnared in the shame in which abuse entangles you.

Regrettably, I am a card-carrying member of several taboo societies of abuse: verbal abuse, physical abuse, a variety of sexual abuses, psychological abuse with impressive longevity, and even creative sexual and mental torture. It's a thick wallet I carry, yet recently, one by painful one, I have examined the numerous stories that have constituted my initiation into clubs that I never asked to join. I hate that I belong here. I hate that I have so many sordid tales of pain and abuse. I'm enraged that my life has been somewhat defined by the sick ambitions of others. I'm angry that I am still struggling to rewrite the opinion I have of myself that was originally penned by monsters. I loathe many things about the obstacles and challenges of healing, but what I can proudly say is that I no longer hate myself, and at 37 years old, that feels really good.

I reached a pivotal point in my life shortly after my own daughter celebrated her eighth birthday. Checking on her late one night, after she had fallen asleep, I was reflecting on the quick rate at which her young life was going by. My only daughter was already eight years old and was the epitome of innocence and delight. Looking at her resting body tucked safely into her pillow-filled bed, I was stricken by her tender age, her small size, her purity. Simultaneously, I was stricken by the recognition of what my small body endured at that very same age. I was horrified. I felt sick. I was overcome by the vivid recollection of the many ways my young body was ravaged by abuse. I wanted to curl up next to my daughter and protect her from the world. I wanted to create a shield around her to ensure that she would never, ever be hurt the way I was. I had no idea that in those moments as I stood frozen next to her bed, I was being catapulted into an excursion of memories that have sometimes felt as dangerous and frightening as when the actual events took place. I finally stepped away from her, breaking my stare at this beautiful, sleeping child that had unknowingly, yet completely, awakened me. I realized that it was time to go back and rescue that eight-year-old inside of me that I had placed in a virtual grave, discarded and abandoned, much like I was made to feel. Thus began my journey to heal.

My oldest sister was often in charge of me. She was supposed to look after me and make sure I remained safe in the absence of my parents. She was five and a half years older than me. She was also immensely cruel and indescribably jealous. By definition, I suppose she did technically watch me. She *watched* as her teenage boyfriend belittled me. He teased me and berated me. He humiliated me and she did nothing to stop him. He made me take my shorts off. He lifted up my shirt and laughed. He slapped me across the face when tears came to my eyes. She *watched* in the doorway of my own bedroom while he pushed me to the hardwood floor and crushed himself into me. She looked on with piercing eyes, a hauntingly callous, unsympathetic look, and she did nothing to stop him. Nothing. I was only eight years old, and this was just the beginning.

At eight, I knew very little about my own anatomy, and having only sisters, I knew even less about males. I didn't know what a penis was, what it looked like, or how it could be used as a weapon that equally destroys little girls and grown women. I had no idea what sex was and certainly didn't know there was a name for what had happened to me that terrible June day. But as my life unfolded, I gained an unwelcome education about many definitions of rape. I learned about being mentally overpowered by someone and about being completely controlled by fear. I learned that for a child, fear can capture you and become strong enough to paralyze you, halting your ability to develop normally. Fear can wrap its brawny fingers around your throat and choke you until you unwillingly submit to the demands of that terror. I obediently acquiesced to the far-reaching fear of my oldest sister until I was nearly 20 years old. I am embarrassed to admit this. I still feel ashamed that my resistance wasn't greater or that I wasn't stronger. I am sad that just as I didn't recognize a weakness in her, I concurrently failed to recognize a strength in myself that was silently present all along. Without it, I would not be where I am today; quite simply, I would not have survived.

My childhood was seemingly normal to an outsider. Even today, my parents would likely describe it as such. Of course, one parent was battling his own demons by way of a 12-pack, while the other was absurdly selective in what she chose to acknowledge. I, on the other hand, felt like I was living a bizarre and surreal double life. At home, I lived at the hands and commands of a bitter sister who was crafty with threats and carefully carried out her games of deception and betrayal without witnesses. She demanded (and was subsequently granted) a faithful vow of secrecy. Her malicious, verbal messages of how unwanted and unloved I was were convincing. Her promise to watch me take my last breath of life seemed to be just that— a promise. As a teenager, I didn't question whether it would happen; I questioned when. I became her pawn and she reveled in her ability to punish me by way of hitting, cutting, punching, and choking. She loved to wake me at night with one hand over my mouth and the other grasping my throat. I believe she thrived on seeing the most primitive form of pure and rightful fear in my eyes, a look of wild desperation confirming that she was in control. In the quiet company of my own thoughts, when I lend my attention to these memories as I try to embrace, acknowledge, and accept them, I can still hear her venomous words trying to poison me. I can hear her threats, her demands, and her lies. Thankfully, as I am learning and healing, her thundering words are losing strength and the power of her messages is lessening. One day, her voice will be nothing more than a whisper that I can, and will, ignore.

My sister would offer me rides, thereby helping my parents, but once alone with me, would treat me horribly. She would not allow me to use a seatbelt and would drive erratically, telling me she was going to crash the car and I would be ejected. She would convince my mother she wanted to spend time with me and would promise to take me shopping or to a movie, but she would drop me off and leave. She was always late returning, leaving me alone, often at night, waiting for her. I couldn't call my parents because the repercussions from her would have been unfathomable. So I waited, alone and afraid. Finally I would be picked up and put in a car full of her friends with nowhere for me to sit but across strangers' laps, where hands would grope and fingers would poke.

Her mind games were endless. Sometimes if she saw a mark she had carelessly left on me, a bruise or a cut that was visible, she would wait until my mother was present and, with a voice filled with false concern, would ask, "What happened? Did you get hurt?" I was forced to lie, covering for her because the fear of what might happen if I didn't far exceeded the amount by which I valued myself. She broke my spirit down with ridicule and hatred. Her verbal condescension was so effectively punctuated by physical punishment that I could no longer hold onto the self-respect with which I was born. I believed I was completely worthless, and even today, I am incrementally trying to find value in myself where it was stolen.

The summer I was raped by my sister's boyfriend (an event that has never been acknowledged between us), I was initiated into the aforementioned club of creative sexual torture with a concentration in psychological abuse. I was the casualty of a next-door-neighbor nightmare. We grew up as friends. He was four years older than me, but in a very rural area, my choices for playmates were limited. Our parents were close friends, so it was only natural for us to form some type of relationship. The relationship he established was not at all the one of innocent summer play that I had wished for.

A tree house built by his adoptive father joined our properties and was a common meeting place to pass the long hours of a summer day. Some days, the play was simple and childishly appropriate, but other days, when his prepubescent teenage years were thrust upon him, he decided to thrust himself upon me, and so began the next four years of torturous tree house trysts. Partly because I am still fighting the acceptance of the word *torture* as it relates to my history, and partly because there were collectively many incidents, similarly disturbing in nature, I cannot recount it all here. With a necessity to acknowledge things that still blanket me in shame (a battle I win as often as one's feet touch ground on a seesaw), I will say that I was repeatedly vaginally and anally raped and was penetrated by many other things not meant for bodily entrance. I was forbidden to cry or to look at him (or his friend on one terrible occasion), and he insisted that before I could leave and try to walk home on unsteady, shaking limbs carrying resonating pain, I had to thank him. I had to say "Thank you," and I had to say that I was sorry. *I* had to apologize for being a child with whom he experimented, a child that he unsuccessfully tried to break.

Recently I learned of a connection between my tree house "friend" and an adult male perpetrator who entered more than just my life beginning around age nine. Although I had long believed him to be a family friend, within the past year, I learned that not only was he the adoptive uncle of the neighbor who had tortured me, but also he is also on the National Sex Offender's Registry. Apparently, I was not the only young girl who was coerced into being alone with him, then intimidated and frightened as he painfully explored my body. Clearly, I was not the only one who was forced to pleasure this grown man as he stroked my head and told me what a good girl I was. There were others who may have been before me, and there were obviously more after me. Either he was caught in the act, or some young girl was courageous enough to use that beautifully strong voice that resides within each of us, and she spoke the truths that I still find challenging to say aloud.

Perhaps if the assaults by this trusted adult family friend had been the only things abusive in nature for me, maybe my voice would not have been muted. The truth is, when he came along and chose to hurt me, my young body and mind had already been quite altered by the hateful and hurtful things that others had done. I did not simply allow myself, at eight, to be completely submissive to these horrible acts. I was broken down from an age younger than that, by the damaging power that words and degrading actions have over a developing mind. I was ambushed by fear and enveloped in terror, and as a result, my adult self is slowly learning how to peel off the heavy blankets of shame that I have been buried beneath. The process of healing from the levels of degradation and humiliation that my abuse history delivered has been painful. Repeated indignities and mortification leave powerful messages and physical memories that are incredibly difficult to redefine, but I am trying. With each successful revision of a message or a memory, I feel empowered. It is a gift I am giving myself. More importantly, I am trying to firmly grasp that these atrocities are not my fault; they never were, not even for a moment. It is my hope that one day, I will be free from any self-blame that still threatens to hold me responsible.

The things that were taken from me during these frightening years are things I once believed to be gone forever. However, as I travel this road of healing, I am learning that there is no permanence with which people can rob you. A soul isn't a tangible item of thievery. I still have all the components I started with; many have just been scattered or torn, disheveled and hidden. It is my job, *all of our jobs as survivors,* to relocate, collect, repair, and rebuild the pieces that will make us whole again. It is overwhelming, but not impossible. It is daunting, but not insurmountable. With a belief in yourself, with encouragement and support and, most of all, with hope that you *will* recover, that you *can* mend and that you *deserve* to reconnect with the child in you that you once abandoned, *you will heal.* That child is waiting for a reunion that only we can make when we are ready to face and embrace the moments in our lives that once imprisoned us. As enormous as they still feel, in the end, they were only moments—moments in our predetermined histories that are shaping us into the beautiful people we are destined to become.

I Promised the Children

by Earthlake

I am here today, not only for myself, but to be the voice of a newborn, an infant, and a young man, none of whom can speak for themselves, and I am here to fulfill a promise I made many years ago.

When I was a child, I experienced abuses that no child should have to experience. I felt so totally alone. There was no one I could turn to for help. My perpetrators were those who should have protected me and a group of people whose names I do not know. I was so young when it began that when standing up I was half the size of the adults who were in charge. I was half the size of those who planned my days and nights. I was half the size of those who tore my heart out. I was half the size of those who threatened me and others with extinction. I was half the size of those who choked the song out of me, robbed me of my sense of safety, manipulated my longing to belong, and ruined my ability to trust and feel a sense of well-being. I was half the size. In order for my perpetrators to carry out their agenda, they used those of us who were wholly innocent to do their jobs. They were not even brave enough to do the work themselves.

Today, I am the sole survivor of those years of horror who can recall and feel safe enough to tell the story: my story, and the story of the three who could not be here with me today. I am alive today only because I lived long enough to finally find help. I was able to find help in countless dedicated and well-trained therapists and good friends from whom I could draw strength, commitment, goodwill, and faith until I found a measure of those things within myself. Had it not been for those people's interventions in my life, I would not have made it through. It was only because of the good grace of people outside my family of origin—upon whom I could depend, trust, and come to rely—that I am here today. I am eternally grateful for each and every one.

Recovery is a mighty challenge. It is not for the faint of heart. It requires more from us than we think we have to give, and then some, and yet it still appears that recovery is possible. It takes many years for some of us. It takes determination, unending courage, and a will to keep focusing on things we cannot see—things that we can only dream of—and things that we can hope for.

Many have given up before they could complete their work. I have known those who lost all hope and couldn't hang in there even one more day. I have known many who have not given up, and many of them have gone on to do good things. Through persistence and determination, those who have not given up have shown us and the world at large that they will not be defeated, that they will overcome all the odds and go on to be of benefit to others, just as others were a benefit to them. So many people I have known have walked my path before me and come out of it on top. These people give me inspiration and the belief that no matter what life has in store for us, we can find ways to cope, ways to heal, ways to thrive, and ways to contribute back.

I have lived a far from perfect life. I have lived so many years hiding secrets I thought too horrible to be believed and too scary to give voice to that I have done my fair share of damage to others, as well. The internal pressure, the denial and the lies from my perpetrators, the complete lack of any kind of validation, concern, and help from my family of origin, all contributed to that life. Although I was light-years ahead of my perpetrators and did not perpetrate the abuses heaped on me, I did fall short in many ways I would have liked to have done better in.

Most of my life I made decisions based on fear: fear that originated with the conditioning of my young mind by those who did not see me as a child worthy of love and protection but who in fact saw and treated me as a being ranking lower than a dog, quite literally. This inability on their part to view me as someone other than a projection of the sickest parts within themselves was not my fault. It was, however, my reality and the reality I had to live with and cope with on a day-to-day basis for most of my life.

I have anger. I have anger not only for myself but also for those who never had a chance against the evil that I saw but was told I also must deny. I had so much stored-up anger by the time I was a teenager that it is a wonder that I was satisfied to fantasize about revenge against my perpetrators instead of act it out. I suppose my fear of jail kept me in line when I could have lost control and exacted my own kind of justice, in my own way. I am glad now that I did not give in and lose my way. I am glad I saved myself from years of more abuse and of living life in cells a few feet wide and only a few feet longer.

I have pain: pain that so much suffering exists; pain that the youngest amongst us have so little power and such small voices; pain that so many children grow up in financial poverty, emotional poverty, mental poverty, physical poverty, spiritual poverty, and medical neglect; pain knowing that evil exists and is often in those you are forced to depend upon; pain that there is not enough help out there or enough resources to meet the needs head-on; pain in knowing there is so much potential lost, so much happiness lost, so much creativity lost, so much laughter never to be heard.

I have fear: fear that survivors won't be able to tolerate the enormity of what lies ahead of them to heal; fear that the abusers will outlive and outsmart the survivors; fear that we won't be believed when we finally have the strength to speak our truth; fear that we will be re-victimized over and over; fear that we will be denied our story because someone else cannot stand to imagine it, hear it, or accept that it occurred and in the way that we remember it; fear that others who have not walked in our shoes will walk on by and not give our plight a second thought; fear that we won't imagine a better future, know our gifts, and set our own goals; fear that we won't ever experience the love we so deserve or that we won't be capable of fully loving those we know; fear that we will give up before we get to the light at the end of the tunnel that can guide us back to ourselves and give us a life of meaning and purpose and service to all others.

I have all these things, but I also have hope. I have hope that someday it will be different. That my children will do better than I did. That my children's children will do better even still. I have hope in the resiliency of the human spirit. I have hope in the people who live their lives with integrity, good intention, and right action. I have hope in the heart's ability to grow in love, in the mind's ability to stretch in imagination, and in the soul's ability to take flight. I have hope in the Creator's ability to hold us when we cannot hold ourselves, to see for us what we cannot see for ourselves, and to guide us gently back to our rightful connection while creating the sacred space within which that happens best.

I have so much to say, so many more ideas and words within to share, but for now I have said enough. Now I will rest peacefully for a time. I am grateful for the blessings that have been bestowed upon me. I am happy that a song has begun to sing in my heart, that a brighter future is building in my mind, and that I am now engaged in living out my true purpose here on earth.

Thank you, dear ones, who cannot be here to sing your own song, imagine your own future, or live out your intended purpose. May I never forget and may I never let you down.

The Unrelenting Optimist

by Carlene

Picture this: a tall, gawky girl made completely of elbows and knobby knees, on the sidelines during gym class, watching her classmates run back and forth on the basketball court with delight, literally bouncing up and down on the balls of her feet. This is me in the sixth grade, at the height of a terrible home life where I was sexually abused and beaten into mental submission by my then-stepfather on a daily basis.

That girl, caught up in the moment and bursting with the joy of being alive, is who I was then and who I still am today.

My name is Carlene. I am an unrelenting optimist, and it's a pleasure to make your acquaintance.

To me, growing older isn't about age, it's about becoming your best self. Everybody always says, "If you could go back but know everything you know now, what would you change?" I think it's like using the warp whistles in Super Mario Bros. 3; I wonder if Nintendo was disappointed they put the effort into designing worlds 2 through 7 when everyone just wanted to go straight from 1 to 8.

My fiancé asked me that question the other day, and I told him that I don't think I would take back anything, that I liked who I am now. "But what about the abuse?" he asked. "Wouldn't you undo that?"

There's a loaded question; if I could go back and get my childhood back from the man who stole it, would I?

I often shock people with my complete disregard for social niceties and my lack of fear—or, as I like to call it, my excess of bravery. Is that the price of a lost childhood? To not possess any fear of living my life as fully as I want to? If that's the case, I would call it freedom.

As shocking as it seems to equate ten years of mental prison with freedom—being manipulated, living my life in fear, lying to the faces of the people I desperately wished would save me—when it left my life, it took with it the fear factor.

When I decided to change courses, to start pursuing music again to feed my soul, I heard the same negative shocked reactions, just phrased differently each time. "Well, Carlene, you know how hard it is to make it in the music industry." "Why are you going to Nashville when there are recording studios right here near your home?" "You know that everyone there is trying to do the same thing as you, right?" "But what are you going to do with your business?"

That's where the unexpected benefit from living through childhood abuse kicked in. I am no longer the type of person to listen to what my Sandler Sales training course referred to as "head trash," at least not when it comes to people trying to take a crap all over my dreams. I don't just have dreams, I have *goals*, and I make those goals realities on a regular basis by thumbing my nose at the people who don't "get" what I'm doing and by dealing exclusively with the people who fit effortlessly into my life.

I don't have to explain my goals as though they're indecipherable. I want to share my music with people who appreciate what I have to say. Period. That's the end of it. And at the heart of that statement is the key to self-improvement.

While I can only speak for myself, I will go out on a limb and say that many of us keep our best selves hidden. The quirks and qualities that make us so brilliant and fun to be around are the things we are terrified to show the world. If someone mocks us for those quirks and qualities, they've found our hidden heart and stuck a knife in it.

The way I became free—free from the abuse, free from the fear, free from the inability to find the proverbial cliff and jump off without hesitation—was to make a conscious decision to put my hidden heart on display. Want to see it? Here it is:

My name is Carlene and I am totally uncool. I have big feet, size 11, and my toes are long, which grosses me out. My right boob is bigger than my left, and I wear push-up bras so no one can tell. I think I am technically 5 feet, 11 and a *HALF* inches but I lie and tell people I'm 6 feet tall because that half inch is *just* more interesting. I had braces for two years and my left front tooth still sticks out farther than my right. When I laugh, I actually "guffaw" just like Goofy. I have scars up and down my arms from cutting myself as a teenager, and I am embarrassed when people stare at them. I hate when there is a "w" pronounced in food—"fewd." I secretly wish I could stop playing guitar while performing, because I'm not very good at it, and also so I could have long fingernails again. I had acne F.O.R.E.V.E.R. and I still get zits at 26 years old. I went through high school believing everyone hated me...then I got Facebook and got real. I love to listen to my own songs but don't want anyone to know, so I hit the "Next" button on my iTunes so the play count stays low. I believe in the Universe the way that some people believe in Jesus. I secretly love the Twilight series and Nora Roberts' novels. I would put a Darwin fish on the back of my car but don't want my car keyed.

There you are. There's my hidden heart. Stab away, I'm not ashamed, because even with my secrets out I am still an unrelenting optimist, and it's still a pleasure to make your acquaintance.

In My Own Skin

by Melanie Cleary

Got up today; I said "Good morning" to myself
Sat on the porch watching the day awake with myself
Stretching my arms and trying to breathe
Well I'm living my life just how it should be

chorus
Because I'm strong enough to be exactly who I am
I'm awake and alive in my own skin
And it feels right just living my life

Living your life and speaking your truths
Is the only way to know that
Right NOW is all we are
Because tomorrow isn't promised to anyone on earth
That's why I am saying today

I'm strong enough to be exactly who I am
I'm awake and alive in my own skin
And it feels right just living this life

Going to bed saying "Good night" to myself
Under the sheets
Cuddling up
Getting warm with myself
Soon I'll be dreaming some dreams
And saying some prayers

Hoping I'll wake up with one more chance to live
And say

I'm strong enough to be exactly who I am
I'm awake and alive in my own skin
And the man on the moon
Is singing along with the tune in his head
Saying

I'm strong enough to be exactly who I am
I'm awake and alive in my own skin
And it feels right as he says "Good night."

Curling Clouds

by Vikram

It was a while back that the streets in the capital city were mostly empty. Especially in the housing colonies, which had roads that slipped in and out, where rows of houses almost identical waited for people to float in and out. A cycle was a common vehicle for children, allowing them to whiz by from lane to lane. Neighborhoods changed with changing people, producing a quality of movement. The vast sky did not change but the clouds curling away always did.

Memory is strange; it brings emotions, feelings. Call it what you may, memory brings the need to repeat, revisit, play out the trapped items living in the hippocampus. A child on one of those days in the past was looking at the sky while cycling. He did not see the mouth of the road that had a few older boys standing, looking at him. The sky always gave him pleasure, as did the trees. It's how he escaped, shooting his thoughts high into the sky with images that his brain made up.

The cycle was suddenly stopped. The child came back to the earth with a flat thud, hearing the voices of boys he knew. They were his classmate's elder brother and the elder brother's friends. They told him that he should not boast about his T-shirts if they came from America. They told him he would be bashed up and sent to America to be made again.

The boy was brave; the sky made him brave. He said something rude. The older boys made him get off his cycle. They pushed him to the lamppost. The classmate's brother came close and whispered, "Come to the house at seven. We are playing a game, and if you don't come, we will hang you from this very lamppost."

The boy felt fear for the first time in a long time. His eight-year-old body shuddered, and his mind made him see his own hung body on the lamppost. He felt the elder boy's fingers on his chest—cold! He shuddered, and he looked up at the sky and saw some clouds pass.

The game they played was strange! Who can remove all their clothes and stand in a circle without fear. A coin would be tossed. Names would be called. Other older boys had joined the group. The younger boys present were made to sit in the circle, the older boys on the outside. The coin was tossed. A boy's name was called first. "Do you feel fear? You will get over it, if you remove all your clothes, including your pants," the classmate's brother called out. The boy looked at his classmate, who just looked back.

The shirt came off.

The shorts came off.

The underwear, tiny and white, was going to come off, when there was a sound of a car.

The group scattered...

The shrink looked at me and asked, "Then what happened with you and your classmate's brother?" I looked up from the paper where I had jotted all of the above.

"He had many games like that, in a dark room where you had to feel the parts of the body and guess what parts they were. So eventually he felt me. He used to hold my testicles, and push his fingers in my anus, in one of the games."

"Did you tell him no? Push him away? Call for help? How old was he?"

I looked out of the shrink's window; I could see the sky and the dark clouds curling away.

"I did not feel so much to like or dislike. I think I was afraid, but later as I grew up a little more, I was asked to stroke my cousin's body, because it made him feel good on those hot days. My fingers went down on him. Then later he made me go down on him. He was much older.

"Then there were many after that. Some forced me. Some I liked; some I was willing to do; some I was not. I like sex with men. I long for love, maybe with a girl who will give me love. But perhaps I won't be able to have sex with her. I don't know."

I was bored.

The shrink was silent.

"Did you tell your mother when she was alive, or your father, about all that has happened with you?"

"No!"

"Why not?"

"My father is still an angry man. And even then, he was. My mother was always angry with me for not studying or something. I don't know! She caught me masturbating with a boy once and once on my own, when I was 12. She said I came from a good family; people don't do these things."

"Why did you not tell her that you were forced?"

"Was I forced, I don't know!"

"What was your relationship like with your mother? Tell me more."

"It was, well, nice; she was kind, hot-tempered, a disciplinary. It has been 23 years since she killed herself. She was never happy, though sometimes I saw her singing to herself. My wish was that I could have saved her."

"How could you? You were 12. Is it not a big responsibility that you have on your shoulder of saving her, especially when at that time you were 12? Is that why you feel you should rescue people from their pain?"

"Perhaps."

"Do you feel if you were with a woman, she would leave you? Like your mother did?"

"No, I am not afraid of loss now, but maybe in the past, yes. However, I feel I won't be good enough for her. I feel dirty. I feel there are cockroaches in me. Women are pure; they are emotional. They don't think of sex like we men do."

"Do you think of sex all the time?"

"No. Only when I feel sad."

"Then after the act of sex, if you do decide to have sex, what happens to your sadness?"

"I feel worse."

"Then why do you think you have sex, presuming you don't like sadness and it makes you feel worse?"

"I don't know. For that one moment, it makes me feels good."

"What does make you feel really good in life other than the moment of sex? We will come back to the ingredients of the act later."

"Well, looking at the sky makes me happy. I like watching the clouds curling, an empty long road, the vastness of an empty field while passing by in a train or a car."

"Can you close your eyes and feel all the things you have mentioned?"

"I can."

"How does your body feel when you imagine you are on the cloud, floating, feeling it, deeply breathing into your spine, hearing your mother singing the song she used to sing to you? What was her favorite song?"

"'Que Sera Sera,' whatever will be will be."

"Hear it in your mind."

I felt the tears begin. Is this what a shrink does, makes you cry, makes you go back into memory and its shards, makes you feel again a fragment of broken glass stabbed into the heart?

The session ended soon. The street was filled with people. The trains were crowded. But in all of that activity, thoughts buzzed like a swarm of bees, sucking the honey from me. I felt at that moment that all my world might explode. I needed air. I was going in circles—nowhere in particular.

I reached a football field and sat down. I saw many legs run around, kicking a football. I felt breathless. I felt lonely. I felt dirty. I felt nothing. I was empty.

At that moment I looked up, and there was the sky so vast and me underneath it—a speck underneath all that sky, a speck that was me.

Then everything became calm.

My outstretched hands felt the sky in my palms, and I knew many things would change, just like the neighborhoods, even though the sky would remain the same, with its curling clouds that change shape but always remain the same.

They would remain as curling clouds.

Later that week, the shrink listened to me describe my relationship with the sky and clouds, and he smiled.

standing naked

by Hadiyah Carlyle

i remember

being called into the principal's office
with the school psychologist
telling him why i wrote the paper
what happened in the early mornings
at 1500 munn ave

i remember
being told i was lying
and never to write again

i remember
resisting
standing naked
before school authorities
wanting to write
wanting to shout
but words came down on me

i remember
all the devices
to make me forget
       electroshock
stretched out on the table
counting 10-9-8

strapped down
an aide on each side

i remember
screaming
no...no...no...
please god
hear me
shock didn't take
doctor called in
orderly's voice
she won't go out   increase voltage

i remember
passing out

i remember
my innocence lost
in my own home
in my own bed
no...no...no...

i remember
the lonely nights
staring out the window on munn ave
our elm lined street

i remember
years later
the winter days
climbing to the top
of alaska king crab boats

working with my hands
in bellingham, washington
i was a welder

i remember
looking down
men leering
the chill
hey lady,
watcha got for me

and—i remember
my body
on cold hard mornings
frozen,
a woman
now
coming
to
life.

The Best Boy

by Dale Coleman

"You are the best boy"
That's what they'd say
As if that would make
All the pain go away

Even today
My mother has lied
Says I was the best boy
'Cause I never cried

Didn't she see it?
He'd take me away
Into the backyard
To have it his way

I was only like five
When all of this started
"Grab onto your buns
and get your ass parted"

I was much too small
For this guy I surmised
Better learn how to fool him
Or be pulverized

So I learned a neat trick
After he'd tried this sometime
Press my thighs tight against it
And wait for the slime

Of course didn't always
Work as I planned
With him so much stronger
The pain I'd withstand

And when he had finished
More childhood destroyed
I'd keep my mouth shut, 'cause
I was the best boy

Freedom

by Forest Emily Franken

I used to dream about tornadoes. In these dreams, I could always sense when one was coming so I'd watch the sky and wait. Until, inevitably, its shape twisted down from the darkness that anchored it. And then, before fleeing, I would take its picture. Because I wanted proof.

Thirteen weeks ago, when I was in Virginia for my friend's funeral, real tornadoes touched down around me for the first time. Like the rape that rearranged me this same weekend, they came and went without revealing their full shape.

I didn't see him coming. Drugged and raped, I only watched when gaining consciousness for brief moments.

Two days later, as the Virginia tornadoes left a nearby hospital in ruins, I searched through the window of the plane to see if I could discern the tornadoes from all that was their backdrop. Isn't what gives them away that which is pulled into their force? But my camera was useless, because I couldn't see them. Just like two mornings earlier, when my only evidence from the rape was the aftermath that I had become.

It's been 95 days since the storm began. Today it raises me high and then sets me down gently with a phone call from the City Clinic. It says, "Your test results have come back negative."

I had them draw my blood 12 weeks from the day. Wondering, still, about the full picture of what the rapist had left behind.

I float up from the news, another layer of shadow passing.

I cancel therapy because I don't want to talk about it.

I land at the café patio where, moments later, a pigeon lands. She's aggressive.

Wanting food. I watch her. I see that her feet are bound by some wire or twine. Bound together.

She pulls one foot as far from the other as the twine allows. I alert the people at the neighboring table to the situation. They look at me with creased foreheads and half-smiles, then continue eating. I go inside the café and ask for a pair of scissors.

She's hobbling across the terra-cotta tile when I return. I ask the man eating pancetta if he'll help. He says as long as he doesn't have to touch her. And I agree.

The first time I was touched, non-clinically, after the rape, was at choir practice. Though I was afraid of sharing inappropriately, I felt compelled to name it. Knew it would be a betrayal not to. Because it was the truth. And since the rape had left me without a center, without borders, without trust, self-worth, or even a sense of self I could recognize, truth seemed to be what was left. The choir was the first circle I told. A circle made of women who sing at the bedsides of the dying. The night I told them, they sang to me.

"She's whimpering," the man says as he nears the pigeon. We're stalking her now. She seems panicky. She flaps to get away. I stop, but the man continues. Now he's holding his jacket out like a net. I advise, fruitlessly, against this. As he pounces toward her she escapes to the nearest rooftop. Feet still bound.

The man returns to his seat and I go back to the café. This time, I come out with a bagel. I tear it to pieces, which I lay across the table. Then I wait. When I mistakenly follow the wrong pigeon, a café patron points this out. I return to my perch. And wait again. This time, when a pigeon lands on the table, I take time to let my eyes focus. The twine is there. This is definitely her. She pecks wildly at the bagel while the man and the patron call out suggestions. But I'm not hearing them. Something in me has gathered. Something pre-devastation. It's making my choices for me. I slip out of the chair and circle her with quiet crouched steps, scissors parted. And from behind, easing the blades into that fretful space between her toes, I cut her free.

Rebirth

by Bryanna Houston

I myself am and could be your daughter, sister, niece, granddaughter, friend, girlfriend, or even your wife. Unfortunately sexual assault happens anywhere, anytime. It knows no age, race, or socioeconomic status. With sexual assault, for the most part, the perpetrator is someone we know.

I was 20 years old and a sophomore in college. I had my whole life ahead of me. Maybe I was even a bit naive. Then I was raped. My whole world and outlook changed that night. I was raped by an acquaintance who was giving me a ride that should have taken five minutes, but it didn't. I should have followed my gut instinct, but I didn't. In my mind, it was five minutes. What can happen in five minutes? It was a couple of hours later when I finally got home. My friends had been calling, looking for me. Luckily, they were there for me when I did get home and convinced me to go to the hospital to get checked out. Although it was a difficult experience, the hospital was more traumatic than I could have imagined, given the state I was in.

Know that this event affected not only me but also all of those around me, including my family. In fact, my whole family was wonderfully supportive and loving through this.

My mom stayed by my side for nearly two weeks, only sleeping when I slept, which was not much. Considering every time I closed my eyes, I was constantly reliving the assault over and over again. My mother and I would sleep in the living room together. Imagine being a 20-year-old adult and not being able to even go into the bathroom by yourself because you are so terrified of being by yourself. That was me. I was no longer the strong, independent daughter my parents raised. I was now like a child who needed her mother with her at all times.

One of my brothers completely lost it when my mom told him what had happened to me, and when she told him that the medication he had picked up at the drugstore was HIV medication. He was afraid to hug me. He did hug me, but the look on his face said it all. He was upset and scared, too.

I am the oldest in my family, where the job requirement, as in any family, is to lead by example. This is not the example I wanted to set for my siblings. They saw me completely differently than what they had been accustomed to.

My family and I were also faced with the fact that I could have contracted a sexually transmitted disease like HIV. I had to get tested and go on medication in case I did have it. It took over a year to be medically cleared, and I am happy to say that I didn't contract HIV or any other sexually transmitted disease.

The friends and family I had around me were great. The truth is I didn't know how anyone else would react. Never mind telling people I was raped, I couldn't even say the word. It was a few years before I could say the word "rape." I was ashamed even though I did nothing wrong. I was embarrassed by what people might think of me, feeling that it was somehow and someway my fault.

This is the same reason I didn't go to the police or prosecute. This is why we need to change the attitudes of people, and in particular men, so that survivors like me don't have this fear. Sexual assault is still such a taboo. We see it on the news but no one knows who the survivor is—of course with good reason. But why should we live in fear like that, when we did nothing wrong?

There is no set response to sexual assault. Everybody deals with traumatic events with different emotions. I went through every possible emotion: shame, fear, hopelessness, anger, and self-blaming. No emotion was off limits. I even had flashbacks. All that kept going on in my head was: What did I do wrong to deserve this? Why me? Why didn't I follow my instinct? It was like a broken record. I knew I had to toughen up and get over it, like many had said to me. I tried. I tried to forget about it and go on with my life. It is just not that easy.

It was not until 2004, after my brief marriage fell apart and the world as I knew it was crumbling in on me, that I realized that I needed to take care of myself and come to terms with being raped or I was never going to be okay.

I had an emotional breakdown and ended up hospitalized for a week. When I got released, I knew that I was going to get the counseling I needed, which I did. My father was there for me every step of the way. He had to be my guardian in order for me to be released from the hospital. I was 25 years old at the time.

I sought counseling services and I am better for it today because of the help I received. There are still some lasting effects of the assault that will always be with me, but for the most part I am okay.

It took two years of counseling. I first went to the rape crisis center. I had an amazing counselor there. I knew I wanted to give back to the crisis center. I was finally getting my life back. I went on to finish college.

In 2007, I was ready for the chance to give back. I became a medical advocate to be there for survivors in the hospitals. I never wanted another survivor to have the experience I did. I also became a survivor speaker to show people that I am a person and I survived.

I have the most amazing family. They were there for me when I needed them the most. I may have been an adult, but I will always be my parents' child.

On the anniversary date of my rape I used to take time out and do things I love to do, and at the beginning my mom would stay home with me, just in case. It is my rebirth day. I will never forget that day for as long as I live. I will never be the same as I was before I was raped, but I am okay with it. I am stronger.

I Am From

by Cynthia

I am from a place not far enough away

Of longitudes of need
and platitudes for hugs

I am from lies and shut eyes,
Booze and flattery
I sit on laurels and laps

I am from weak stock
though they hid it well
Kings in the Corner,
They hid me well

I am from a zipped-up code
and a legacy of winks

I am from deluxe crayons and woods out back
I hopscotch truth, I dance for them all
And Solitaire, lots of Solitaire

I am from starry breath and
pails of prayers for fairness
I am from crack-less sidewalks—lest any backs break.

I am from swollen redness.
Memories gestate, staggering to care

I am from curtsies and flippant scripture,
polite talk needing drinks refilled

I've changed my name, but am still unsafe
From a clearinghouse of humanity, the red-dot specials
I want medals *and* monuments

I am from a place
where security changes all the time
And protocol frustrates
I need a past to re-enter

With such fickle coordinates, I rarely visit where I'm from
My wishful itinerary and laden baggage wait

With thanks to George Ella Lyon

Wisdom's Past

by M. E. Hart

Through the gray darkness
Through the godless hell
Through the rain of tears
Through don't tell
don't tell
Through endless fears
Over the razor's edge
Through suicide's garden
This I pledge...

To know my love as deep as my anger
To stare into the eyes of darkness face-to-face with danger
To understand the causes of all of my fears
To uproot, slash, and burn that soul-wrenching terrain clear
To search deeper than the surface when life's triggers appear
To go beyond understanding when someone I love has been speared
To stand tall and not flinch
when daily bias pricks my skin, again and again
To never question the truth my heart tells
even when friends don't hear my truth well

To reclaim all   stolen   parts   of me

To spend my life, every second I have left, free

Free from patterns that steal my joy
Free from the hatred in the eyes that silently call me "boy"
Free from the chains media images re-make
Free from it all

This freedom I now know I must take

I learned hard-knock lessons in the gray darkness
I learned of life's evil living through the godless hell
I learned of life's pain through the rain of tears
I learned of the terror in silence through don't tell, don't tell
I learned of lost strength facing the endless fears
I learned delicate balance walking over the razor's edge
I learned there's no pain worth walking back through suicide's garden

These are lessons of wisdom's past
        I intend to live them now hard and fast...

Some of our contributors wanted to share additional information about themselves, while others preferred only to share their writing. Below are the biographical sketches of those contributors who chose to be included in this section.

Deb Sherrer is a writer, yoga instructor, licensed school psychologist, and activist in violence prevention. She lives in Shelburne, Vermont, with her husband and daughters. Her writing has been published in *The Burlington Poetry Journal, The Mountain Troubadour, Affilia, Violence Against Women International Journal,* and *Hope Whispers.* More of her essays and poems can be read at www.debsherrer.com.

Andrea Harris teaches women's studies and English at Wright State University. She is the cofounder and faculty liaison of Survivors Offering Support (SOS), a network of female survivors of violence at Wright State. In addition to offering a safe space for survivors to share stories and strategies, SOS also hosts inclusive campus events to increase awareness of violence and provide opportunities for empowerment and healing. Andrea regularly speaks to diverse campus organizations and classes about her research on and personal experiences with domestic violence and sexual assault. Her personal work with survivors takes her to homes, hospitals, mental health facilities, police stations, and courtrooms. Her roles as survivor, mother, writer, teacher, scholar, and activist live in concert with one another.

M. E. Hart used journaling and poetry writing to heal from childhood sexual abuse. He is completing work on a book, *Living 2 Thrive,* which will help teach other trauma survivors those same skills. Hart is an attorney with 15 years of experience working with professionals to improve critical social and emotional intelligence communication competencies in the corporate, government, and not-for-profit sectors. He currently works as a vice president for a consulting firm in the Washington, DC area. Hart dedicates his contributions to those who survive and strive to thrive.

Elizabeth McCurry is a freelance writer and a survivor of childhood sexual abuse. She expresses her healing through her writing and art. She hopes her poems and artwork will help others on their road of healing. She is now happily married with two beautiful children, who are her motivation to continue on her road of healing.

Dale Coleman's neighbor moved in next door when he was four or five years old and began sexually abusing him. He quit talking at age five or six and did not begin talking again until the neighbor moved away when Dale was eight or nine and in second grade.

Jennifer Majesky is a graduate of Nazareth College in Rochester, New York. She works as a child advocate at McMahon/Ryan Child Advocacy Site in Syracuse, helping children who have been sexually and physically abused. She is thrilled to be making her published debut with Safer Society Press.

Kitty Garn lives with her son in Columbus, Ohio. In addition to working full-time, she is also completing her BS in human development and family sciences at Ohio State University with an eventual goal of obtaining a master's of social work. Kitty is active with an organization that provides advocacy for survivors of sexual assault and hopes to continue, through her writing, to raise awareness of the many serious issues facing American women and girls.

Richard G. is a 50-year-old interior designer who works and resides in New York. He has been clean and sober for 12 years. He enjoys making and exploring new connections that allow him to be who he was meant to be when he was born.

Jolie McKenna, MS Ed, received her bachelor's degree in history and philosophy from Marquette University in Milwaukee in 1984. While working on her master's degree, Jolie worked in a diverse number of social justice environments, from Milwaukee Municipal Court to the House of Corrections in Franklin, Wisconsin, as well as a community support program for the chronically mentally ill in Milwaukee. After obtaining a master's degree in adult education from the University of Wisconsin, Jolie joined the State of Wisconsin Department of Corrections as a parole agent for 12 years. After leaving the state, she returned to adult education. Jolie wrote the poem "Boundaries" while managing a prevention services program for a domestic violence prevention agency in Kenosha, Wisconsin. She is honored to have been included in this collection.

Julia Vileisis is currently attending Virginia Commonwealth University for her undergraduate degree in psychology. Upon graduation she will enter the Medical College of Virginia. She plans to become a child psychiatrist.

Peter Wien is currently in his early 60s and works in the field of market understanding of the green consumer for a company called Earthsense, LLC. He is the caretaker of a parrot that he is planning to reintroduce into a contained flock after 15 years of it flying wild in his house. His interest in art, nature, and the planet are core to his life. His struggle and healing from his experience are always there. Their effects change continually. He lives in Connecticut and Denver, Colorado.

Susan S. Russell, M.A., has extensive experience working as a victim advocate and currently serves as a consultant for the Office for Victims of Crime. Susan has often been invited to speak on the subjects of victimization, survivorship, victims' rights, and restorative justice. She may be contacted at russells@madriver.com.

Jon lives and writes in the Carolinas.

Marcia lives in New York with her husband and son. She is a psychotherapist and movement therapist. One of her specialties is working with incest and physical abuse survivors.

Linda Schritt is a registered social worker. She has worked in the helping profession for over 20 years. For 10 years, Linda worked in the field of family preservation and support and then as a contracted sexual abuse counselor for a nonprofit organization. She has since written a book, titled *Walking the Crooked Mile,* which guides abuse victims in working through the healing process.

Rebecca left California to return to her hometown in Alabama to serve as a school counselor and health education teacher. She also worked for the local rape crisis center as the prevention educator. During this time she spoke publicly about her own experience. She now works in the accounting field and takes in horses, which have always made her feel complete. She remains very active with the rape crisis center.

S. Kelley Harrell is the author of *Gift of the Dreamtime* and *Awakening to the Divinity of Trauma*. Her shamanic practice is Soul Intent Arts. She is a founder and co-president of the Saferoom Project (www.saferoom.org), a nonprofit online peer support network for adult survivors of child sexual assault.

Mitzi Soto Albertson lives in California and is currently enjoying her 49th year. Memories of her abuse did not surface until she was in her 30s, but once she understood them her past actions and feelings made more sense to her. She always wanted to be a writer but lacked the confidence to try. After she began group therapy, the words just poured out of her without much prompting. This release of words triggered a similar release of past pain and heartache. She is honored to share her words with the hope that they can offer some solace to others who have survived similar experiences.

Desmonette Hazly received her Ph.D. in international politics and policy from Claremont Graduate University and is president and CEO of Odissi International, LLC. Odissi International (OI) is an economic and community development corporation committed to "Building a Better World Responsibly" and focuses on economic and community development strategies that promote corporate and consumer integrity and mutual benefit. Dr. Hazly has a B.A. in child and family studies and holds master's degrees in social work and international studies. She has studied abroad and received diplomas in culinary arts and has studied extensively at the Cordon Bleu in Paris and London.

International experiences as a liaison for UNICEF, a U.N. representative for issues on family violence, and the director of international services of the American Red Cross, Los Angeles chapter, inspired Dr. Hazly to explore meaningful ways to connect with cultures and create an environment where multicultural learning could successfully exist. In her international travels, Dr. Hazly continuously expands on her skills and has greatly influenced education practices globally.

Beth Smith is the author of over 200 poems and a novella. She has additional work touring the state of Virginia with the Virginia Sexual and Domestic Violence Action Alliance. She hopes that her poetry can inspire other women to leave abusive situations and rediscover their voice.

Sabrina Francesca Manganella lives in Savannah, Georgia, with her husband, Jack Simmons, and her two daughters. She is working on a book of essays and photographs chronicling her quest to live large while recovering from childhood trauma. She is pleased to say it has a happy ending.

Liz Cascone is an anti-violence advocate living in Richmond, Virginia. In her spare time she enjoys writing poetry and painting.

Nazneen Tonse, 44, is an Indian writer and artist who began healing from her childhood abuse experiences in her late 30s. The therapeutic process made such a difference in her life that she decided to share her what she learned with other survivors. In 2002, she ended a 15-year career in corporate advertising and moved from Bahrain, the land of her birth, to settle down in Bangalore, India. Over the last eight years, she has worked on developing several online resources for and about adult survivors of childhood abuse. These resources, titled The Askios Projects, include a Web site, blog, and online groups (http://askios.tripod.com). Askios is personally managed and funded by Nazneen and is not a registered NGO (non-governmental organization). It is one of only two resources in the nation that are exclusively for adult survivors.

Kathy is a natural creative channel who shares her gifts with the world through her poetry, writing, and energy work. She touches people in a deep way during her candid and conversational presentations. She is also the founder of Inner Journeys, which provides tools, techniques, and products that enable personal transformation and healing on all levels. She is currently writing her memoir, *Up from the Ashes.*

Jackie is blessed to have two amazing daughters. They light up her heart and soul. She is grateful for the love of her life, who sees and loves her whole self. Her mother, brother, and sisters are like breath to her. Donna, knowing you and "What She Knows" has transformed me. Jackie is honored to be a part of the healing for trauma survivors whether she is therapist, educator, consultant, or survivor. Although she continues to face shame, it lessens as Jackie lives more and more in her body, with her breath.

Sara lives in Michigan. She is a graduate of Western Michigan University. Sara worked as a secondary teacher for 18 years in Michigan, Illinois, and the Washington, DC area. She currently works in the mental health field.

Paula Hodgkins grew up in rural Maine. She was educated at the University of Maine and Northeastern University, where she attained a master's degree in technical and professional writing. She currently works as a technical writer in the Boston area and lives a quiet life with her two cats.

Mary Zelinka has been involved in the movement to end violence against women since 1980. She works at the Center Against Rape and Domestic Violence in Corvallis, Oregon, where she witnesses the remarkable strength and resiliency of survivors of sexual and domestic violence every day.

Melanie Cleary is an author and violence prevention activist, currently residing in northern California. Melanie considers herself not just a survivor but a thriver, having survived child abuse and molestation, family violence, domestic violence, and several sexual assaults. She is very proud of her nearly 13 years of personal empowerment and healing. Melanie is most grateful for the opportunity to have found her place and voice, working within the violence prevention movement for the past seven years, and looks forward to a world free from violence and abuse.

Vikram was born in October 1974 in the state of Gujarat in India. He graduated in 1996 with a degree in English literature and went on to get a master's degree in sociology from the Delhi School of Economics. He went on to complete certificate courses in art-based therapy, hypnotherapy, and theater development. He has worked in the development sector for 11 years. His work entails using creative processes for human development and the use of creative arts in the process of empowerment of marginalized communities like runaway children, homeless youth, and transgendered people. Vikram loves teaching, training, and communicating with groups of young people in the areas of sexuality, sexual abuse, gender, HIV, and psychological safety. He has a keen interest in writing and has written several workbooks. He is also interested in theater and has directed several plays. Working with groups of all kinds is both his passion and his profession.

Hadiyah Carlyle says she is now old enough to be a "part of history." In the 1960s she was a single parent in Haight Ashbury, San Francisco. In the 1970s, she was a shipyard welder. She's working on her memoir.

Forest Emily Franken completed an M.A. in dance/movement therapy and an MFA in choreography before moving to the Bay Area in 1998 to receive training in a contemplative discipline called Authentic Movement. For the past 10 years, she has worked in psychiatric hospitals while studying and teaching this practice. Through her clients and personal experience, she has become deeply curious about the power of a good-enough witness to assist in the transformation of suffering.

Bryanna Houston was a medical advocate from 2007 until 2009 for the Boston Area Rape Crisis Center because, she says, she never wanted another person to go through what she had gone through and not have someone else there for support and understanding. Since 2007 and until the present day, she also has been a survivor speaker throughout eastern Massachusetts.

Cynthia is an incest survivor with PTSD. She experiences somatic memory; she does yet not know what happened to her. Her recovery process includes daily yoga, psychotherapy, pelvic physical therapy, writing, and painting. She attributes group therapy as the most important part of her healing thus far. She wishes great self-compassion, courage, and patience to all on their unique healing journey.

Resources

If you are an abuse survivor and are looking for resources to start your own healing journey, here are a few organizations that may be able to provide support and assistance. Safer Society Foundation and Safer Society Press do not specifically endorse or recommend any program. This listing is provided as a service only.

Adult Survivors of Child Abuse (ASCA), www.ascasupport.org, is an international self-help support group for adult survivors of neglect or physical, sexual, and/or emotional abuse. Survivors learn to transform their self-identities from that of victim to that of survivor and, ultimately, thriver. The site includes resource materials and guidelines for establishing ASCA support networks.

Childhelp National Child Abuse Hotline (1-800-4-A-CHILD) is a free 24-hour anonymous telephone hotline providing support to kids, as well as adults concerned about kids, who are experiencing abuse or neglect. The Childhelp Web site (www.childhelp.org) includes a learning center that provides resources for children, parents, and professionals.

The National Domestic Violence Hotline (1-800-799-SAFE) is a 24-hour telephone hotline providing support to anyone in a domestic violence situation as well as an online resource (www.ndvh.org) for topics on domestic violence, sexual assault, battering intervention and prevention programs, working through the criminal justice system, and related issues.

The National Sexual Assault Hotline (1-800-656-HOPE) is a 24-hour telephone hotline and an online hotline (www.rainn.org), both operated by the Rape, Abuse, and Incest National Network (RAINN). The secure Web-based hotline provides a safe and anonymous place for victims to get help online. RAINN also works to promote education and prevention of sexual assault and compiles and shares links to legal resources, including the state mandatory regulations regarding children and the elderly.

The Office for Victims of Crime, www.ojp.usdoj.gov/ovc includes a Web page of resources on incest and sexual abuse.

Safer Society Foundation
and Safer Society Press

The Safer Society Foundation, Inc. is a private, non-profit agency working to end sexual abuse and its detrimental effects on society. We believe sexual abuse is a public health issue whose solution can only be found in an integrated, system-wide approach. To this end, we seek collaborative partnerships with treatment providers, the legal system, mental health agencies, survivors, educators, parents—everyone with a stake in this crucial issue.

Safer Society Press is the publishing program of the Safer Society Foundation. Please visit the web site to learn more about other Safer Society Press titles, including several titles for survivors of abuse.

P.O. Box 340, Brandon, Vermont 05733
802-247-3132
www.safersociety.org